TEXAS COLLECTS

TEXAS COLLECTS

Fine Arts, Furniture, Windmills, and Whimseys

Paul Nathan

Foreword by James A. Michener

Taylor Publishing Company
Dallas, Texas

Book Design by Juanita Barnes

Published by Taylor Publishing Company
1550 West Mockingbird Lane
Dallas, Texas 75235

Library of Congress Cataloging-in-Publication Data

Nathan, Paul, 1913–
  Texas collects : fine art, furniture, windmills, and whimseys /
Paul Nathan ; foreword by James A. Michener.
    p.   cm.
  ISBN 0-87833-554-4 : $45.00
  1. Art—Private collections—Texas. 2. Antiques—Private
collections—Texas. I. Title.
N5216.T4N38 1988   88-10182
707′.4′0164—dc19   CIP

Printed in the United States of America

0 9 8 7 6 5 4 3 2 1

For Ruth
who magically
made it happen

CONTENTS

FOREWORD

When my wife and I moved to Texas for an extended work session in 1982, we were delighted to have an opportunity to glimpse, now and then during our travels, the caches of art that were hiding in various corners of that huge state. It seemed that each sizable town had a collector of Western paintings, or American primitives, or European examples, or fine canvases and sculptures by contemporary American artists. There is hidden treasure in Texas and when the day comes, perhaps in the early years of the next century, that these fine works find their way into public museums, Texas will have a stunning display of first-rate art.

In the meantime, there are excellent museums already available. Whenever we had the chance we stopped at Fort Worth's exquisite Kimbell Museum, which must be one of the loveliest in America. Located close to the Amon Carter Museum, a repository of Western art, the Kimbell is an architectural gem designed by Louis Kahn of Philadelphia. It provides as harmonious a setting for art as we have ever seen, and the relatively few paintings it contains (as compared to museums like the Mellon in Washington and the Metropolitan in New York) are of top notch quality. To visit the Kimbell is to be reminded of what art is and what a museum should be.

When we started our pilgrimages, Dallas—much bigger than Fort Worth—had no major art museum. But during the years we were there, Dallas built one of the outstanding museums of recent years, the Dallas Museum of Art, a masterpiece in size and with the capacity to do great work in the future. For the present it has only a limited amount of first-class art to display, but when the private homes begin to disgorge, as they will, Dallas is going to move into the class of Kansas City, Detroit, and Seattle, and, perhaps, even surpass them.

The Museum of Fine Arts in Houston, founded in 1924 as the first art museum in the state, was always under repair when we visited it, but we never failed to see something rewarding and exciting. I am told that plans are underway for consolidation of its holdings and expansion to accommodate new acquisitions, which will make it first class. Certainly the energy to accomplish this is available.

But there were three other museum-type operations in Texas that gave me great personal delight. Someone lacking my interest in history and language might not enjoy them as I did, but I would be delinquent not to mention them. The Harry Ransom Humanities Research Center at the University of Texas at Austin contains a miraculous collection whose extraordinary quality is widely known. It is an assembly of perhaps the finest examples of English literature extant outside of Great Britain. Early editions of Chaucer, Shakespeare, and John Milton are part of this rich storehouse, and manuscripts of famous authors of the nineteenth century are abundant. To study writers like D.H. Lawrence, James Joyce, George Bernard Shaw, and T.S. Eliot, scholars must go to Austin for their research. To accompany this wonderfully rich collection, the center also has assembled a fine gallery of portraits of great writers unsurpassed in America.

In the little town of Plainview on the western prairie is an unpretentious museum, handsomely arranged and documented, showing what life on the great plains was like during the heyday of the American cowboy. The Panhandle Plains Historical Museum avoids gimmickry, seeks authenticity, and specializes in meaningful exhibitions. It is a little treasure, and a writer like me hopes that museums half as good will rise in various parts of the United States depicting the salient features of life in those regions.

But the Texas museum I love most is unique in America, so far as I know. In the Panhandle city of Lubbock, on the vast campus of Texas Tech and part of the Texas Technological University Museum, is the Ranching Heritage Center, a collection of more than twenty authentically restored buildings depicting the story of West Texas ranching through the early 1900s. Houses, barns, stables, windmills, and other buildings have been moved here at considerable expense from all parts of Texas. The assemblage as a whole illustrates what life was like in the last century and early half of this.

Of course I am aware that groups of buildings like this have been assembled elsewhere in the East, South, and West, but what makes this one unique and doubly valuable is the manner in which it is displayed. The founders, realizing that they could never afford to house such a collection or even roof it over, brought huge bulldozers onto their prairie and gouged out a small depression for each of their buildings. The earth thus collected, the same bulldozers moved it into protective ridges around three sides of each building, giving it isolation, individuality, and protection from storms. Each building is in its own earth-bound museum, and the effect is magical. I learned in Lubbock that such man-made earthen ridges are called berms. Well, hidden among the berms of Lubbock there is a treasure.

Because Texas collectors have not yet given their treasures to public museums at the rate New York, Boston, and Philadelphia owners have done, I do not want to specify certain private owners who have minor museums of their own; but I will recall one visit among many to the home of a husband and wife who owned what they said was a modest group of rather good canvases. They had one each of Renoir, Manet, Gauguin, Van Gogh, Monet, Braque, and at least half a dozen others of like merit.

Understatement may not be a characteristic most people associate with Texas, but it does exist there—along with practically everything else.

James A. Michener

INTRODUCTION

The late Marietta Kleberg would recall how, as a child, she once said something that made people laugh, though at the time she didn't know why. She was the daughter of Richard Kleberg, Sr., who had married into the King family of King Ranch fame. Asked by a kindly gentleman, "Little girl, where do you come from?", she replied, "King County, Texas." The gentleman wished to be further enlightened: "And where is that?" "In Grandma's northeast pasture," said Marietta.

This story came often to mind during the course of researching and writing the present book. Texas's sense of scale is different from most of the world's. Further, the enormous wealth generated by oil, land, and cattle has fed the conviction of citizens of the second largest state that to them all things are possible. Collectors in Texas have tended to operate with a prodigality—sometimes a profligacy—that sets them apart even from others of their special breed.

Accepting a collector's important gift, the spokesman for a large institution serving the public said, "This is what it means to be Texan—the element of reach. Texas's reach is supreme over all others."

It was the "element of reach"—the ebullience, the panache, the bred-in-the-bone self-confidence—that made the idea of an illustrated sampler of Texas collectors and what they collect appealing to both the author and the publisher. The original impetus for undertaking such a project, however, was sparked in 1984 when H. Ross Perot was prepared to pay $70 million to take over the Museum of the American Indian, located in New York, and relocate it lock, stock, and barrel in Dallas. That created quite a stir in New York and all around the country, a stir which confirmed in us the growing sense of the importance of Texas as a preserver and promoter of cultural values. We recognize in Texas the energy and zest that a hundred years ago were concentrated in the eastern part of the country.

Although fine arts are extensively represented in the following pages, they constitute only part of the picture. Included too are native American artifacts, gold coins, rare books, folk art, antique furniture, guns, classic cars, theater memorabilia, beaded whimseys, old TV sets, barbed wire, pottery, spurs. If it exists, be assured someone in Texas has collected it.

To attempt to produce a complete survey of Texas collectors and collections would be futile, and the result, if it could be achieved, would be a bore. For starters, museums of various types number in the hundreds. Scores of these are old jails preserved with their historical appurtenances. There are the many art museums, from which a small selection has been made here. There is also a fascinating Texas Rangers Museum in Waco with such assorted attractions as a barbed-wire collection, examples of buffalo-horn furniture, and melancholy personal mementoes of Maximilian and Carlotta, the Austrian archduke and his wife transplanted into Mexico with fatal consequences. And how can one ignore the museum featuring wax likenesses of all the winners of the annual Miss Texas competition? Happily there already exists an excellent guide, an invaluable *vade mecum* for anyone ''doing'' Texas museums: *Texas Museums* by Paula Eyrich Tyler and Ron Tyler (University of Texas Press, Austin, 1983.) Our policy in these pages has been to deal with museums only to the extent that they have grown out of, or provide space for, personal collections. Thus, tempting as it was, the Alamo, for example, with so much history on display, was found to lie outside the book's framework.

Coverage of personal collections in private homes is less than exhaustive, for several reasons. First, there are a great many of these collections, some more noteworthy than others. In certain instances where one might have liked to include a personal collection, the collector has chosen to avoid the publicity, having been advised that it could drive up the insurance premiums, or simply being fearful of word getting out about a houseful of treasures.

The variety and strength of corporate art collections in Texas is impressive, but we reluctantly decided that most of them could not be linked to the personal ambition of individual collectors.

The first collector we examine is, as the chapter heading says, quintessential: through Miss Ima Hogg we are led into the special world of the serious Texas collector that is the province of our book. Succeeding collectors and their holdings are grouped in five categories: ''Personal and Private'' describes collections not seen by the public; ''Private Goes Public'' treats those that started as private collections but subsequently have been opened to all; ''Personal and Public'' includes collections that in some measure meet both criteria; ''Pro Bono Publico'' feature collections that from the start were intended for the public; and finally, ''The Museum Makers'' is concerned with collectors of art whose undeviating pursuit has led to the outstanding museums validating their visions and doing honor to their names.

TEXAS COLLECTS

THE QUINTESSENTIAL COLLECTOR: MISS IMA

If any one person can be said to have set the style for collectors in the state of Texas, it might well be the late Ima Hogg.

She started collecting almost three-quarters of a century ago, and was already acquiring early American furniture and decorative objects of highest quality before most people recognized their real value. Although it is on American antiques that her reputation rests, she also bought American Indian artifacts and works on paper by artists in the European vanguard at a time when there was little demand or competition for either. Furthermore, in later life she undertook the rehabilitation of a pioneer Texas community, "collecting" and relocating old houses to be incorporated into the restoration.

Everyone who has ever heard of Ima Hogg must speculate about her name . . . and the parents who gave it to her. Some people said that not only was there Ima; she also had a sister named Ura. Not true. Ima's siblings were brothers: Will, Mike, and Tom.

The real story about Ima seems to be that she was tagged after a fictional character dear to her father, though there are differing explanations of where the original is to be found. One version suggests that the character appears in a novel by Sir Walter Scott; the other, that she is the heroine of an epic poem, *The Fate of Marvin*, written by Ima's uncle. Perhaps he, too, took his inspiration from Sir Walter.

Whether or not there was a literary source, it taxes credulity to believe that the name could have been bestowed without some less-than-benign intent. James Stephen Hogg was a three-hundred-pound oil and real estate man and populist governor of Texas from 1891 to 1895. When his chronically ill wife died after the end of his tenure in the governor's mansion, Ima already was accustomed to filling in as his hostess. She continued in this role for the rest of

The gardens become increasingly less formal as the grounds dissolve into a woodland setting.

Ima Hogg's Bayou Bend, designed in 1926 by Houston architect John Staub, combines elements from a number of famous American houses, chief among them Homewood, a country house near Baltimore built in 1803. The exterior of the Classical Revival mansion is stucco and painted pink, Miss Ima's favorite color.

17

The curly maple highboy in one of the bedrooms at Bayou Bend is dated 1790. A stenciled border of pineapples and the tree of life are typical colonial symbols.

Hogg's life. A photograph taken at age eighteen shows her to be comely and graceful, and we know that her mother, a woman of sensibility, had encouraged her talent for music and her pleasure in fine clothes. Endowed with an outgoing personality, Ima displayed no overt signs of a scarred psyche. On the contrary, she appeared to be someone who knew how to enjoy herself; and, to be fair to her father, he treated her like a person of consequence, entrusting her with a mature woman's social responsibilities, taking her with him when he traveled and instilling in her an interest in history, horticulture, education, politics, and public services.

Miss Ima, as she was familiarly and fondly known, was active in many areas during her long life (she died at ninety-three in 1975.) A pianist, she studied at New York's National Conservatory of Music and also in Munich. She was one of the founders of the Houston Symphony Society in 1913 and later its president. Undergraduate courses in psychology taken at the University of Texas ultimately bore practical fruit with her establishment of the Houston Child Guidance Center and the Hogg Foundation for Mental Health. She also participated with her brothers in the management of the family oil and real estate holdings.

And she collected. "It is said that collecting is a dis-

ease," Miss Ima once confided. "I think I had it from childhood." In 1917 when she was thirty-five, she made what may have been her first purchase of antique furniture, four chairs, all English: a Chippendale armchair and side chair and two Adam side chairs. Within three years her taste turned to American decorative art. It took a certain sophistication in those days to see that American antiques might be more rewarding than British for the serious collector. The finest English furniture had been made for the nobility and upper classes and emphasized embellishment, often lavish. On the other hand, much early American furniture of top quality was more simple, intended primarily for utility in a society still setting up housekeeping. For those in the colonies who wanted it, and could afford it, there was furniture closely imitating the high-style creations left behind.

In 1973, looking back on her collecting career, Miss Ima observed, "The Bayou Bend collection was always designed for the public. From the time I acquired my first Queen Anne armchair in 1920, I had an unaccountable compulsion to make an American collection for some Texas museum." (Presumably, the armchair was one of those crafted in America, in English style.) During the twenties, while continuing to buy American furniture, she purchased early American glass, Tucker porcelain, and the work of native artists, notably a *Penn's Treaty* by the painter-preacher Edward Hicks. By the fifties her vision of a museum had come to include a series of complete rooms incorporating examples of the various kinds of decorative arts in a unified whole.

The house known as Bayou Bend that now serves as this museum was not intended as such when it was built in 1927. It was meant to be the home of Miss Ima and her two bachelor brothers, Will, eight years her senior, and Mike, three years younger. A two-story, pink stucco mansion with porticoes, it is in what might be called Latin Colonial Style. Miss Ima threw herself into the planning, working closely with a local architect, John Staub, and ending up with something that, in spite of its twenty-two rooms, is unpretentious and inviting. It is situated on fourteen acres in Houston's choicest residential neighborhood, River Oaks, bordering Buffalo Bayou, a winding brown stream. With their magnificent plantings of azaleas, the gardens are as much an attraction every spring as the house's interior.

During the 1930s Miss Ima scaled down her collecting. Will had died as the decade opened, and family and business affairs required her attention, as did the gardens, still in process of being laid out. When she had time to collect, however, she bought Southwestern jewelry, kachina dolls, and Native American pottery. Meanwhile she cultivated a new-found interest in Russian avant-garde artists and such Western contemporaries as Matisse, Chagall, and Picasso. She came to own, and later transfer to the Houston Museum of Fine Arts, works by these and fellow Modernists. Also, in due course, she added late-nineteenth- and then eighteenth-century American paintings to her holdings, which eventually included canvases by John Singleton Copley, Gilbert Stuart, Charles Willson Peale, Samuel F.B. Morse, and a Hicks *Peaceable Kingdom*.

After the end of World War II, when Miss Ima once more began to acquire furniture, she found that other collectors in increasing numbers had climbed aboard the early-American bandwagon. Good pieces now were scarce and, consequently, more expensive. Feeling that in this contracting market she could use expert and professional guidance, the pace setter in the field sought out top Eastern dealers and museum curators and formed alliances with them that lasted for life. She also became friends with other prominent collectors. Friendship did not, however, preclude rivalry. She enjoyed nothing more than beating out Henry DuPont, for example, on a rare and beautiful Chippendale corner chair made in New York around 1760. Earlier she had snatched a set of eight perfectly matched Chippendale chairs and a matching chairback settee from under his nose. No wonder that Bayou Bend, except in

In Miss Ima's upstairs sitting room are splendid examples of Queen Anne furniture.

Architectural details in the drawing room reflect the neo-Palladian style of the late Georgian era. The portrait of George Washington was done by Gilbert Stuart and is part of her collection of 18th-century American paintings.

scale, comfortably holds it own against DuPont's grand Winterthur in Delaware.

It was in great measure due to the influence of her friends that Miss Ima came around to the idea of converting her home into a museum. After DuPont opened his residence as a "house museum" (a term of his own devising), he and others encouraged Miss Ima to do likewise. Among collectors of a certain stamp there tends to be fellowship. When Miss Ima made up her mind to buy a rare Newport tea table directly from its owner, she turned to Houston banker Charles L. Bybee to handle the financial arrangements. Bybee and his wife, Faith, also were redoubtable collectors of eighteenth- and nineteenth-century American furnishings and early Texas pieces.

In keeping with her plan to furnish and decorate whole rooms in an authentic manner, Miss Ima began to acquire pewter, glass, silver, and ceramics. As with everything that captured her interest, she read the books and con-

sulted with the authorities in each field, until she herself was an authority. Certain rooms have descriptive names. The Texas Room features the relatively simple furniture of the settler era together with a large collection of mid-nineteenth-century transfer-printed earthenware in the Texian Campaigne series commemorating the Mexican War. There are Massachusetts and Newport Rooms and a Federal Parlor. The Belter Parlor displays rococo revival settees, chairs, and tables, all intricately carved. The furniture came from the New York City workshop of John Henry Belter, who in the mid-nineteenth century was America's preeminent cabinetmaker. By a patented process employing steam heat, he molded solid wood. Laminated, these ended up stronger than solid wood. The Belter furniture in the Bayou Bend parlor is complemented by a white marble fireplace, ornate chandelier, and assertively patterned upholstery, wall covering, and rug. The overall effect is one of Victorian excess.

Left: The dark blue paneling of the Massachusetts Room sets off the collection of Chippendale pieces from that state.

Right: An elaborately canopied bed, a Boston corner chair, circa 1785, and a bombe desk furnish the Chippendale Bedroom.

Miss Ima had been buying Belter since the 1940s, when there was almost no demand for it. Even when she gave it a room at Bayou Bend, some of her collector friends still considered it unworthy of its surroundings. To Manhattan antiques dealer Harold Sack, who was unenthusiastic when shown a piece she had purchased, she said, "Harold, there's the future. You'd better get with it!" As usual, time was to vindicate her judgment. Within a decade Belter was commanding steep prices.

In contrast to the rooms organized to set off the furniture and decoration of a particular locality, one drawing room blends examples from various places. Thus visitors are able to compare and perceive differences in design, workmanship, and materials characteristic of Philadelphia, New York, Newport, and Boston.

In a house filled with treasures it is difficult to pinpoint the most noteworthy. However, a painting of particular charm is a triple portrait, dating from around 1788,

by Charles Willson Peale, for whom George Washington frequently sat. (Bayou Bend's Washington portrait is one by Gilbert Stuart.) In the Peale, the artist's self-portrait is centered on the canvas, with his wife Rachel seen in a painting-within-a-painting and his young daughter, Angelica Kauffmann, depicted reaching behind him to touch his brush. Like her three brothers, Raphael, Rembrandt, and Titian, she too was a gifted artist.

There are two other Gilbert Stuarts, also four American portraits and five English drawings by Copley, who spent his last years in London.

A block-and-shell tall secretary, dating from Revolutionary Newport, adroitly combines pine, mahogany, cedar, and chestnut and exhibits architectural details of uncommon refinement. A rare high chest of a type made in Boston before 1750 is japanned to simulate oriental laquer. Decorative birds, flowers, deer, and teahouses have been applied in gilt and gesso against a background sugges-

A collection of 19th-century glass is displayed in the Pine Room; the box on the table typifies 17th-century English beading and stumpwork.

Right: Bayou Bend houses Miss Ima's personal collection of American antiques, which, until 1920, had not been considered valuable when compared to its European counterparts. The Chillman Parlor is a showcase for furniture from the American Empire period, 1810–1830.

tive of tortoise shell. A simpler but very handsome burled William and Mary high chest can claim a distinction of its own in being veneered on the sides. The all-but-universal custom was to confine the veneering to the front, since the sides of such a piece are not visible to the casual eye; in this case the instruction obviously was to spare no expense.

A mahogany card table believed to have belonged to Peter Faneuil, remembered for Boston's pre-Revolutionary Faneuil Hall, boasts its day's latest custom touches. A folding framework hinged to the back legs opens to form an extension of the table's skirt—an effect known as concertina action. The top of the table is covered with tambour work.

white salt-glazed stoneware, pottery from Edgefield, South Carolina, and from the Newcomb Pottery in New Orleans. Paul Revere and John Coney were among the silversmiths whose work she sought out. The list of acquisitions could be extended. It seems safe to say that few objects in the house are without story or significance.

A close friend, Nettie Jones, once saw Miss Ima off by train to Boston. "She went all the way to Boston and back," she told a reporter after Miss Ima's death, "just for one glass bottle."

At the dedication of Bayou Bend in 1966 Miss Ima said, "Texas, an empire in itself, geographically and historically sometimes seems to be regarded as remote or alien to the rest of the nation. I hope in a modest way Bayou Bend

Above: The front entrance to the estate, now a museum operated by the Museum of Fine Arts, winds through acres and acres planted with azaleas.

Left: The Belter Parlor displays rococo revival settees, chairs, and tables, all intricately curved, from the New York workshop of John Henry Belter, America's preeminent cabinetmaker by the mid-nineteenth century.

The embroidery's durability is matched by that of the Irish stitch upholstery, still intact, on a Chippendale wing chair made in Massachusetts some time in the second half of the eighteenth century.

Upstairs in Miss Ima's sitting room there are splendid examples of Queen Anne furniture. During the Queen Anne period (1702-1714) there was a movement to eliminate gratuitous ornament. Sarah Duchess of Marlborough spoke for the Queen when she voiced a desire "to have things plain and clean, from a piece of wainscot to a lady's face." For daily living, Miss Ima clearly shared the ideal of simple, unostentatious surroundings.

Always fond of ceramics, Miss Ima collected English delftware of the late seventeenth and early eighteenth centuries, mid-eighteenth-century Staffordshire mottled ware,

may serve as a bridge to bring us closer to the heart of an American heritage which unites us."

Miss Ima had quit her house for an apartment the previous year. With her farsighted vision she understood that there could be opportunity for the collection to grow after her death. She preferred that this happen through the efforts of motivated individuals, cultural organizations, and corporations, so she did not establish an endowment for acquisitions. As she hoped, the community from time to time has made valuable contributions. A masterful still life of vegetables by yet another member of the Peale family, James, Charles's brother, and portraits by Rembrandt Peale and Thomas Sully enrich the holdings in American painting. A handsome New York sofa, circa 1810-1830, Grecian in style with gilded dolphin supports, adds one more distinctive piece of furniture that Miss Ima herself, given the opportunity, surely would have bought. Comparable purchases or gifts of textiles, works on paper, metalware, ceramics, and glass have filled in gaps or augmented existing strengths.

PERSONAL and PRIVATE

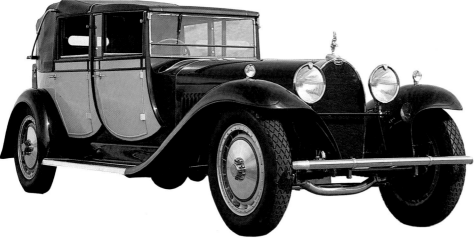

PERSONAL and PRIVATE

The Immodest John Jenkins III

On Christmas Eve, 1985, fire roared through the corrugated-iron building on Interstate 35, outside Austin, that housed what was probably the world's largest stock of rare books for sale. When the embers had cooled at The Jenkins Company, it was found that the flames, and to an equal degree smoke, had caused enormous damage. Destroyed were not only books but precious oriental rugs, art works, and antiques with which the interior of the ugly yellow structure was incongruously furnished and decorated. Further, the entire stock, equipment, plates, and supplies of the Jenkins Publishing Company, another enterprise of John H. Jenkins III, had been wiped out.

The fire was believed to have been started by a short in an electrical extension cord. Tallying the losses in antiquarian collections, Jenkins listed 250,000 government publications, more than 10,000 Texana titles (the most extensive such collection in private hands), 8,000 state histories, 7,000 books on economics, 3,000 on petroleum, entire collections of Western history, botany, music, and art, and large numbers of items from Civil War and Latin American collections. Lost, too, was a recently installed computer system. With the exception of certain rare books insured as collateral against bank loans, nothing was covered by insurance.

Yet John H. Jenkins was not completely destroyed. Approximately half a million volumes, including the most valuable, kept in two vault rooms, were spared. Although obliged to scale back his publishing operation, he has continued to function at full tilt as a dealer. Also, being a collector, he had many priceless works safe at home at the time of the fire.

Jenkins can trace his collecting proclivities, as well as financial acumen, to childhood. Born into a family that for several generations seems to have just missed or fumbled opportunities to strike it rich in oil or real estate, he began to make money in the rare-coin business when he was about nine years old. He did this by going to the bank every Friday afternoon and exchanging larger denominations for small change—up to thirty dollars worth. By Monday he would have picked out a few coins that dealers would pay him for, sometimes a penny bringing four or five dollars. By the time he was ten he was able to set himself up as the Southwestern Investment Association, doing business through ads in coin collectors' magazines.

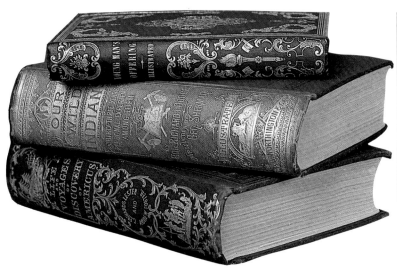

Despite a fire in 1965 that destroyed hundreds of thousands of volumes, Austin dealer and collector John Jenkins still maintains one of the world's largest inventories of books, notable among them a collection pertaining to the West and Southwest in the eighteenth and nineteenth centuries.

He even rented his own booth at national coin shows; but at thirteen he switched to antiquarian books. One reason for this change was his early childhood desire to be a writer, specifically of nonfiction. To succeed, he figured, he would need a reference library. He has always considered himself a collector before a dealer; his purpose is still to build the best possible library, particularly in the areas of the Texas Revolution and Republic of Texas, his main interests—but in order to pay for the books he collects, he must sell others.

In 1975 he staked his claim to the title of world's biggest dealer in his field by buying out Edward Eberstadt & Sons of New York. This brought him some 40,000 rare books and manuscripts for which he paid around $4 million. By 1983, sales from the Eberstadt takeover enabled him to pay off the bank loan with which he had made the purchase, and the remaining stock was then found to have appreciated in value to about $16 million.

The bulk of the Eberstadt collection pertained to nineteenth- and late-eighteenth-century history in the West and Southwest. Among Texas highlights were Stephen F. Austin's 1833 plea for the separation of Texas from Santa Anna's Mexico, a 1774 census, and a priest's account of missionary work and exploration in the early eighteenth century.

Jenkins and the University of Texas in Austin enjoy a symbiotic relationship. The university's Harry Ransom Humanities Research Center has one of the greatest libraries in this country or anywhere else; Jenkins has sold it thousands of books, and the research center frequently turns to him for appraisals of material from other sources.

While he was in high school, John Jenkins wrote a book based on memoirs left by his great-great-grandfather. It was published the day he graduated by the University of Texas Press, with a foreword by the then dean of Texas popular historians, J. Frank Dobie. Jenkins went on to obtain a degree in history from the university. He has since spent 14 years compiling a bibliography, *Basic Texas*

Books, a 650-page guide to the essential titles for a reference collection about the state.

"I believe no one has read more Texas books than I, with the possible exception of Professor Eugene C. Barker of the University of Texas, and he's dead," Jenkins says. Before he trimmed his bibliography to its present 224 entries, it had included some 1,300. Even in his enthusiasm for his subject, Jenkins had to acknowledge that a volume containing so much information would be inordinately expensive to publish or purchase, and that few people could afford or give shelf space to all the recommended works. *Basic Texas Books* was printed by Jenkins' own press.

There are still more strings to the Jenkins bow. As a real estate entrepreneur, he paid more than a million dollars in 1977 for an abandoned cluster of decrepit buildings—formerly Trinity University, then Westminster College—in Tehuacana, near Mexia in eastern central Texas. The rehabilitated campus and plant now produce income as a conference center.

Jenkins is also a crime buster. When a stranger offered him examples of incunabula and "big pictures of birds, American birds," which could only be Audubon prints, and even hinted that books could be stolen to order, he asked him to come back later. Knowing that word of the prizes already purloined would have circulated among his colleagues, he made the right phone calls and learned who had been victimized. Then he flew to New York, ostensibly to close a deal. His meeting with an armed member of the thieves' ring was broken up by the FBI, which he had tipped off. The episode, with fictional trimmings, later turned up on the television series *Kojak*.

And Jenkins is a show business angel. He backed a lurid low-budget comedy-horror movie, *The Texas Chainsaw Massacre* which has surprised a lot of people by becoming a cult classic and box office bonanza.

Jenkins once informed a reporter, "It has never bothered me to appear immodest." Judging by the record, there is no reason it should.

The Newest Antique

Anyone who shares the popular belief that television came in with the 1940s would be startled to see Bernard W. Sampson's collection of early TV sets. Some of his choicest pieces date back to the late twenties and early thirties. And the older they are, the more futuristic their appearance. In anticipating the present day, the pioneer designers gave free reign to imaginations strongly influenced by the science fiction and Dick Tracy-type comic books of their era.

Sampson, a young Houston artist, once collected vintage radios and semi-antique toys, among them plastic, wood, or tin motorcycles and riders, space craft, space stations, and robot figures. He built and sold, as he still does, large robots, more than eight feet tall, which play music or talk or function as cabinets for video screens. But the nature of his collecting changed a few years ago when he was faced with having to furnish a new studio. Scouting Houston's antique shops, he came across a 1949 Art Deco bakelite General Electric television set. Though non-operative, it pleased him, esthetically. He bought it, planning to restore it.

"I thought it would be fun to have a 1940s set working in the studio," he says. "I started thinking about it, and started making some calls. I found there were a lot of interesting old television sets around." He grew so involved in tracking down and buying these that he never did repair the first one, although he has had a number of subsequently acquired sets returned to useful life by a local restorer.

A native of Houston, Sampson attended schools in Arizona and London and received instruction in kinetic art at a college south of Dallas. Back once more in Houston, he was married for a time to Shelley Duvall, who was clerking at a department store when some Hollywood people interested in seeing Sampson's art discovered her and gave her a screen test. The test led to a contract and the couple moved to Los Angeles. They divorced and Sampson, still drawn to Houston, found inexpensive space there where he could live and work. Taking up residence on the second floor of a warehouse and remodeling it to meet his needs, he became a leader in the urban rehabilitation movement that has been converting Houston's NoHo Artists Warehouse District into a kind of scaled-down version of New York's SoHo. Harking back to his kinetic art studies, he started turning out his larger-than-human robots while also creating multimedia works and children's books, both text and illustrations.

In the course of assembling his present collection Sampson has educated himself in various aspects of television's evolution. He owns sets representative of most successive stages. The most venerable among his inventory are mechanical examples with small neon tubes in place of today's picture tubes. In these primitive models, shifting configurations of light behind a spinning, perforated wheel projected an image through a magnifying lens, often onto a mirror. Screens on the very oldest sets were all small and round, though the roundness might be disguised by framing. Many of the sets were assembled from kits by the purchasers; some had video but no audio, the sound being supplied by a radio receiver.

Although it is commonly assumed that all early picture tubes were small, this was not invariably true. The first picture tubes had very long necks. Thus, to avoid the tube's sticking out into a room, it was encased in a tall cabinet. Dumont in 1950 manufactured a 30-inch black-and-white tube that is still the largest ever made for black and white.

American and foreign brand names, some still current, others superseded, share the spotlight in Sampson's collection: Spartan, Stewart-Warner, RCA, Zenith, Sony, Baird, Marconi, General Electric, His Master's Voice (*La Voix de son Maître* in a French model), Echo, Leningrad, Dumont, Stromberg-Carlson, Admiral, Emerson, Motorola, Philips, Scott, Viewtone, Transvision, Pilot.

Sampson acknowledges gaps in his collection. For instance, he does not have a set with what the Soviets claim is the first picture tube, said to have been invented in Uzbekistan, Tashkent, circa 1927. (Quite possibly no other collection has one either.)

And he lacks statistics regarding the number of pre-World War II sets remaining in Russia, which was thought to have produced roughly one thousand.

"The Soviets had electronic television earlier than the

The tall, narrow, mirror-in-the-lid
television—1936 Baird from England,
using a 15" picture tube set vertically in
the cabinet and viewed from a hinged
mirror.

U.S.A.," he says. "RCA helped them set up the first station in Moscow. Also, the Soviets had the first woman commentator."

Prior to World War II 5,500 electronic TVs had been manufactured in the United States. The distribution of those surviving is estimated at approximately 100 in this country, 100 in England, and another 100 held by collectors elsewhere. Sampson owns 23 sets of pre-World War II vintage, which he believes makes his coverage of that era the third most extensive anywhere. Overall, counting in his other 188 sets, Sampson claims the world's second-largest collection.

The Germans say they introduced the first regularly scheduled TV programs in 1935. Hitler for some reason never appeared on television; nor, according to Sampson's research, did the Führer employ TV for propaganda purposes, only for entertainment. After the occupation of France, all French radios and TVs were confiscated and television shows were beamed from the Eiffel Tower, mostly to German soldiers in hospitals. About 400 mechanical and 400 electronic TV sets belonging to the French were destroyed by, or hidden from, the invaders. Very few examples are believed to have survived.

Both in Germany and the Soviet Union television viewing was restricted at first to public places; sets were not sold to individuals. In 1938 and 1939 the Leningrad, a tabletop model, went on sale and theoretically could be bought by anybody. Sampson believes that between 300 and 500 were disposed of but doesn't know if any still exist.

Of three clear Plexiglas sets made by RCA for exhibition at the New York and San Francisco world's fairs in 1939, none is known to survive. If one were found, it would be worth many thousands of dollars.

Sampson describes the major challenge he set for himself as a collector: "I have friends in the Soviet Union," he says. "One is a mathematics professor at Leningrad University; another is an American woman who attended university in Moscow, married a Soviet student, divorced him and lived for a while with their child in San Francisco. She went back to the Soviet Union and became a citizen. She works for the *Moscow News* and has connections. My friends are going to try to help me hunt down early Soviet television sets. Then I'll try to get them out of the coun-

try." He adds that he believes there would be nothing illegal about this.

Television sets have been called "the newest antiques," and as such are beginning to whet the interest of many potential collectors. Sampson warns that pre-World War II sets have grown so scarce and the prices so high that they are now beyond the reach of most people. Post-World War II sets are rising in price as well, some bringing as much as $1,500. Householders who have neglected to clean out their attics since the late 1940s or early fifties may find dusty treasures among the debris.

The large television-at-the-top—1937 His Masters Voice from England, using a 9" picture tube set vertically in the cabinet viewed through a solid glass magnifying lense from a mirror set at a 45 degree angle. This set also has a 3-band radio and a 78 rpm record player. Only 10 of these televisions were made.

On the Trail of the Earliest Americans

Perhaps it was prescience on the part of the venerable Indian, a recognition that the five-year-old standing before him was destined to become a student of his people's culture and a collector of its artifacts. Or perhaps it was merely routine practice to hand out presents to children. The famous Chief Two Guns White Calf was one of several Blackfoot who welcomed guests to the main lodge in Glacier National Park in Montana, the traditional homeland of the Blackfoot tribe. Hearing that the little boy from Fort Worth was deeply interested in Indians, the tall, dignified old man gave him a small, black rawhide rattle and a photograph of himself, which he signed in pictographs. From the photo it was easy to believe what people said: that Two Guns White Calf was one of the models for the composite portrait on the Indian-head nickel.

"From that day forward I was an avid collector," says Gordon W. Smith. He still has both items, the nucleus of the collection that overflows from the living room of his house to museum-style display cabinets on the floor below. With his family's encouragement, Smith traveled throughout the United States in the 1930s looking for objects. Many were acquired from Indians who remembered the white man's wars. These old-timers were gratified that someone wanted to preserve their heritage in a day when even many younger native Americans seemed eager to assimilate the former enemy's culture.

Smith recalls visiting an aged Lakota (Sioux) woman at Pine Ridge, South Dakota. After they had talked for a while, she offered him her "possible" bag, so called because such bags held everything possible. Hers was ancient, of leather, partly beaded, containing several of her most personal belongings. Among these were an awl, a knife worn down from being sharpened, a small rawhide rattle, and a quantity of dyed porcupine quills in a buffalo bladder pouch. To her these were precious possessions, and Smith was fully aware of the honor of being entrusted with them.

Immersing himself in Indian culture, Smith put himself in the way of unusual experiences. With his family he attended the annual Hopi snake dance in 1934. This took place in Hotevilla in northern Arizona. During the dance, climaxing a nine-day ceremony, the participants carry live snakes in their mouths, both poisonous and non-poisonous. Afterward the snakes are released as messengers con-

Gordon W. Smith of Fort Worth has been collecting art and artifacts of the American Indian since his 1930s childhood. Among his prizes is a beaded buckskin dress belonging to a woman of the Lakota tribe of the Plains culture area. Decorated in a complicated design of thousands of seed beads, the dress was worn to a costume ball at the White House in 1933.

veying appeals for rain to the spirits. While in Hotevilla, Smith acquired a painted rain snake effigy fashioned from a twisted cottonwood root. For several weeks during their travels, the Smiths had seen not a drop of rain, but the day the rain snake effigy was placed in their car it began to pour, and the rain continued all the way home.

Smith's collecting slowed down with the start of World War II, when he went into the Navy. He did, however, pick up a few examples of Melanesian art in the Solomon Islands. Following the war he attended graduate school at Columbia University, earning a master's degree in contemporary British literature and also taking courses in the graduate art school. For a time he worked in publishing, then became an architectural artist, designing and creating sculpture, mosaics, and stained glass.

When he resumed collecting, with Fort Worth once more his home base, he extended his scope to include some examples of pre-Columbian, African, and Oceanic as well as American Indian art. The practice of collecting, Smith finds, becomes more difficult and painstaking as time goes on. "Quality objects are scarce and hard to find," he says. And there's the high incidence of fakery. He cites reports that in the Far East old Indian beadwork is being replicated so perfectly that even the experts can barely tell the difference. Smith's collection reflects American Indian cultures coast to coast. It offers a strong showing in prehistoric objects, and all the areas of cultural significance are represented: the Eastern and Southeastern Woodlands, the Plains, the Plateau, the Southwest, California, and the Northwest Coast. Included are clothing, weapons, musical instruments, ceremonial objects, utilitarian items, basketry, pottery, and games.

Although it is a catholic collection, its emphasis tends to be on the Plains culture, that of the area in which Smith lives. As a cross section of the art and artifacts produced by the Plains Indians after the advent of the horse, the collection is comprehensive. In the eighteenth and nineteenth centuries the Plains Indian culture was based on the white man's horse, and it is one of the ironies of history that the source of the culture was also the cause of its ultimate destruction.

Cultural interaction was not limited to the plains, however, but forms the basis of much Indian culture from the sixteenth and seventeenth centuries on. An example of such interaction from the Southeastern Woodlands is a Seminole man's shirt in the collection, representing a type of clothing generally developed by and confined to the Seminoles. Dating from about 1925, the shirt is an intricate patchwork of hundreds of pieces of brightly colored cloth stitched together on a sewing machine. While the

style of such shirts may have been influenced by Spanish clothing of the eighteenth century, when the Seminoles first moved into Florida, their complex design was probably inspired by early American patchwork quilts. Smith purchased the shirt in the early 1930s from a Seminole Indian in the Everglades, who up until then had been wearing it regularly.

Smith proudly displays what he calls "one of the most remarkable examples of cultural interaction," an Apache violin from the Southwest. Such fiddles are believed to have been the only stringed instruments made by any Indian tribe; the Apaches got the idea after seeing Western violins. Not able to duplicate their shape, the Indians came up with their own design. The violin is constructed from a hollowed-out cottonwood limb, which forms a tubular soundbox about two feet long. This is strung with catgut (two strings) and played with a crude horsehair bow, producing a rather squawky but not unpleasant tone. The instrument is beautifully painted with geometric designs, a departure from the models.

Smith points out that in considering American Indian art it is necessary to remember that, like all traditional art, it has profound ideological significance to the people who made it. Few objects were created exclusively for beauty or utility; to a considerable extent, objects conveyed religious expression, a view of the universe. Whether a war bonnet, shirt, basket, or spoon, each article in some measure embodied the spiritual power undergirding the Indians' existence. A notable example in the collection is a magnificent beaded buckskin dress of a woman of the Lakota tribe of the Plains culture area. The yoke is covered with a complicated design composed of thousands of seed beads. Dating from the late nineteenth century, the dress caused quite a stir when worn to a costume ball at the White House in 1933.

Before beads were available, the Plains Indians created elaborate and beautiful designs from porcupine quills. The quills were first colored with natural dyes—certain barks, herbs, and earth pigments—then flattened by running them through the teeth. The design was created by applying the quills to other surfaces, usually leather or rawhide. Starting about 1830, glass beads made in Venice were brought to America and traded to the Indians, who quickly devised ways of using them. Soon after, beads largely replaced quills as the chief medium of leather and rawhide decoration. The Plains Indians excelled in the new technique.

While Indian design, like that on Smith's dress, had special meaning, the meaning is sometimes elusive. Many symbols were born out of personal mystical visions held by the Plains Indians and to this day remain undecipherable. Others, however, are universal, appearing frequently in Plains Indian art. Small pyramidal shapes represent mountains, and crosses are stars. The entire design, with its deep-blue background and intricate branching forms, may depict constellations reflected in a lake, a rendering of the unity of sky and earth, and of power meant to protect the wearer.

A different sort of protective power was associated with the grizzly bear. A warrior who killed one of these daunting animals earned the right to wear a necklace of its claws. The necklace bestowed upon its wearer some of the characteristics of the bear—its bravery and ferocity—and its protective power. The claws on the necklace in Smith's collection are mounted on otter skin and are separated by trade beads.

One of the most beautiful creations of any tribe is the Osage friendship blanket from the Plains culture area. Smith's example incorporates six human hands against a black background and a border of geometric symbols. It is made from trade cloth—wool and brightly colored silk—and, like the Seminole shirt, was put together on a sewing machine that also had been traded to the Indians.

With justifiable pride, Smith points out his Lakota winter count, or calendar. These were produced by only a few Plains tribes and are called winter counts because the Lakota word for winter is also used for year, winter being the season of greatest concern in a northern climate. The winter count is painted on a piece of buffalo hide. Like all winter counts, it is composed of pictographs that spiral counterclockwise from the center of the skin. Each pictograph represents an event (unique or dramatic, or sometimes bizarre) by which that particular year could be remembered. The man charged with painting the skin decided on a pictograph only after consultation with the tribal council, after which it was added to the slowly growing spiral. Smith's winter count may be the rarest object in his collection, and would be the envy of many museums.

Left: An Osage friendship blanket made of wool and brightly colored silk was stitched on a sewing machine that, like the cloth, had been traded to the Indians.

Even though Rosemary Weatherred's first collection of antique toys was given to a Houston museum because she ran out of room to house it, the need to collect is a compulsion. Whole rooms in her Richmond, Texas, house are given over to antique doll houses and miniatures.

PERSONAL and PRIVATE

Childhood Revisited

Rosemary Weatherred's antique toy collection offers wondrously detailed glimpses of daily life in miniature.

An aunt who died at age fifteen was, and continues to be, an important influence on Rosemary Weatherred, today a grandmother and a widow with a long, full life to look back on. When Rosemary's Aunt Dorothea first became seriously ill as a nine-year-old, the ailing child's father built her a doll house. Family friends from all over the country sent dolls and furnishings to give it life. Although Rosemary was just two at the time of her aunt's death, she has good reason to remember her. "I was the only grandchild," she says, "and when I'd go to visit Grandma she'd bring this box out. Each little thing was wrapped in tissue, and I'd unwrap it and think I'd died and gone to heaven. It was just great! I learned to love the tiny things."

The taste for doll houses and what goes into them has not waned over the years. If anything, it has grown stronger, more compulsive. And the urge to collect has extended into other areas, including toys and art, almost exclusively from times past.

Mrs. Weatherred's late husband Preston came to their marriage with a similar urge. Together they collected antique furniture, decorative objects, paintings (he favored historical marine subjects), and toys. Separately, she collected miniatures such as had graced Aunt Dorothea's doll house, while he went in for early American tools. "The antique toy collecting really got under way," Mrs. Weatherred recalls, "when our children married and let us call our house our own. At the time I was writing decorating articles for most of the home magazines, and I always had to put my typewriter on a card table in the middle of the family room. When the angels left I suddenly found room for a study. I started thinking about how I wanted to decorate it and decided to use a small antique toy collection, thinking it would give a folk art effect. What I didn't realize was that old toys were the best possible examples of folk art, as everything that was made for adults was reproduced in miniature for children."

Well and good, but the toys when first set out for display proved a disappointment. There were not many of them and they were so small that they "looked like freckles on the wall." Needing to enlarge the collection gave the couple a wonderful excuse to explore New England, where Rosemary had family connections. "Every new car we'd get," she says, "would automatically head that way, and we'd stop at every antique shop and junk shop. We didn't

9

know that antique toys were almost impossible to find, much less afford, so we enjoyed beginners' luck and came back with a stuffed station wagon. Instead of toys for the room it was room for the toys, then the whole house for the toys, and finally a museum for the toys."

They acquired and completely remodeled an old house on Montrose in Houston to serve as the Nine to Ninety Antique Toy Museum. The venture was a great success except that they did not own the building and were eventually forced to move the 5000 toys back home. Once again they were faced with the impossibility of housing their entire collection, so they sold the toys for what they had paid for them, and the collection ended up as a gift to the city's heritage society.

Following her husband's death, Rosemary felt the emptiness of their house all the more keenly with most of the toys gone. She had kept just a few that had family associations. "I then told myself," she says, "that if I just collect antique doll houses and miniatures, I'd have ample room for display. That was true for a while, until I got carried away again!"

Eventually she moved to a house in Richmond, about 30 miles outside Houston. Soon she was enlarging the new one to accommodate the seemingly unstoppable flood of toys and doll houses.

Here the human living quarters and those for dolls and toys are pretty much separate, whole rooms upstairs being given over to the latter. Some of the little houses offer wondrously realistic glimpses of life in different classes of society. One elegant residence features a game room with card players seated around a table. Another table near by—approximately two and-a-half by four inches—has a marquetry top designed for backgammon, while in another part of the same salon a man with a cue stick is leaning over a billiard table eyeing a ball, poised for play. A fourth table holds a checkerboard about an inch and-a-half square.

Elsewhere, a man is tubbing himself in a bathroom. The tub, being of the nineteenth century, is on feet. There is a dressing table with mirror, a dry sink holding a wash basin and pitcher, and a commode with overhead flush tank and pull chain (workable when the tank is filled with water).

There are boudoirs, decorated to the last detail, a music room containing half a dozen different instruments, drawing rooms, a child's playroom, small in itself, and loaded with toys, dolls, and games scaled down proportionately. Some houses are set in gardens, fenced in. The houses range in size from the diminutive to those almost as big as a child.

Besides houses, Weatherred displays miniature shops such as were popular at the turn of the century, some of them imported from abroad. A bakery offers candied apples and tempting cakes and pies (a lemon meringue looks particularly appealing). A woman behind the glass-fronted case stands ready to wrap up the goody of your choice. The rotund, leather-aproned butcher in his shop holds a cleaver with which he is about to turn the carcass before him into cuts of pork. Other meats are laid out on a butcher-block table, and fowl hang from hooks. Dogs and a cat patrol with a proprietary air. A greengrocer's shop is stocked with vegetables and fruits that fit into cartons and baskets of thumbnail size. The lettering on a plump bag reads: "Forest Grown Royal Purple Eggplant."

School books from about 1830, magazines for children, miniature books, a Humpty Dumpty circus with clowns and animals, a carousel, tin or lead soldiers—these and more are represented in the collection. Not to be overlooked is a rare assortment of early childhood mugs. Also rare is a set of blocks from around 1870, designed for the construction of churches. Each block is inscribed with a quotation from Scripture, so that the builder will absorb religious teaching during play.

At last count, Weatherred says she had 159 antique dolls, many of them wearing clothes she sewed for them. Clearly, the little people with whom she has surrounded herself have an almost living reality for her. And so too, after short acquaintance, do they for the visitor to their charmed world in Richmond.

The collection's tiny vintage room settings are better than
textbooks at illustrating popular interior design practices of
the day.

Realms of Gold

Along, dark table dominates the library/conference room. It is covered with gold coins, each in a small transparent envelope, aligned in rows across the width of the table. Their quietly proud possessor is Thos. H. Law, of the Fort Worth law firm Law, Snakard & Gambill. He has gone to the considerable trouble of fetching his collection from the bank vault downstairs and laying each precious item out in chronological sequence for the edification of visitors uninitiated in numismatics.

The sole scrap of relevant knowledge the latter bring to this meeting is that Tom Law's collection of English gold coins is recognized as preeminent in the Western Hemisphere. (The world's finest is in the British Museum.)

The trim, erect, white-haired gentleman smiles as he recalls how the seed of his collection was planted in childhood. His father, a university professor, let him keep the Indian head pennies that occasionally turned up in loose change. "There were still a few of them in circulation then," Law says. "Many years later, about five years ago, I had an exhibition of my coins at the University of Texas. One of the reporters was asking me about them, and I told her about collecting the Indian head pennies. When the story came out, she had it as Indian head nickels. I guess she couldn't believe anyone was still alive who had found Indian head pennies in circulating change.

"As I got older my wife and I would travel abroad. Jo Ann would pick up a souvenir of the country in the form of a charm bracelet and I would pick up some cufflinks. Finally I had more links than I was likely to have shirts, so I decided to renew my coin hobby. Eventually I had gold coins from about a hundred countries. At that point it occurred to me there was no way I was going to own them all, so in 1973 I decided to specialize in the coins that to me are the most beautiful, historic, and fascinating, that is, the gold coins of Great Britain. They're fascinating for a number of reasons, among others that, beginning with the reign of Henry VIII, they had very good portraits of each monarch up to the present time, including Elizabeth II. And of course that is the heritage of so many of us anyway, so it was particularly interesting to me to have them."

As to why one collects coins at all, Law reads aloud from an article by Dan Cody he had come across in an airline magazine: "The romance is in that intangible lure

Tom Law, a Fort Worth attorney, has assembled over his lifetime one of the Western Hemisphere's preeminent collections of English gold coins.

of the tangible, the lust for the once was and the might be. The romance is a pirate's treasure, Inca gold, Roman loot and Wall Street wealth, all boiled down into a single round nugget of nothing, were it not for what it represents. . . If every coin is an engraver's masterpiece, it follows that every collection is an art museum in miniature.''

Putting the magazine aside, Law continues, "Gold, of course, has held a fascination for man throughout the centuries, and when you can combine gold with beautiful portraits—especially when the coins are in periods of history one finds particularly interesting . . ." He savors the idea.

"To me it's a marvelous privilege to be able to own and hold in your hand a coin that might have been in circulation in the day of Caesar—and indeed was. I have some from that era. And from before his time. Philip II of Macedonia, the father of Alexander the Great, for example, placed in circulation one of the earliest gold coins, a beautiful stater. This depicted a chariot with horses on the reverse and a handsome Apollo, perhaps with Alexander as the model, on the obverse."

Law turns to the display on the table. Among its distinctive features is that there are two examples of almost every

coin. Thus both the obverse and reverse of a particular piece may be seen at the same time. Law does remove one of each set of coins, however, for his guests to handle and inspect as he describes and places them in their historical context. The English king whose reign marked the introduction of gold coins was Edward III, who ascended the throne in 1327. Law explains that the demand for such coins arose with the need for something more valuable but no bigger than the silver coins already in use for carrying on trade with Flanders (today's Netherlands). Old Greek and Roman gold coins provided a precedent.

The coin between Law's fingers was struck in the aftermath of a naval victory over the French at Sluis, near the English Channel, the largest naval battle in history up to that time (1340). Close to 400 ships were involved and the king himself took part, reportedly engaging one of the French commanders—a lawyer, Law notes with a gleam of amusement—in hand-to-hand combat. The queen and her retinue looked on from a ship off to one side, a common practice in those days, discontinued later for reasons of safety.

Celebrating the English triumph, the coin, known as a noble, carries an engraving of a ship on which stands a king holding a large sword and a shield. In the words of a popular rhyme of the day:

"Four things my noble showeth to me:
King, ship and sword
And the power of the sea."

Around the rim of the coin runs a legend in Latin: "By the grace of God, King of England and France, Lord of Ireland and Aquitaine." Additional lettering on the body of the coin reaffirms that the king was not only the king of Britain but of France as well, an assertion appearing on coins all the way into the reign of George III, hundreds of years after the British monarch had any basis for such a claim.

Following the first hand-struck noble came others of differing sizes, the smaller known as either half or quarter nobles. They were issued over a span now divided into three periods: pre-treaty, treaty, and post-treaty. The treaty referred to was between France and Britain, the Bertigni. While this was in effect, the letters signifying the king's dominion over France were eliminated, to reappear subsequently. He meanwhile retained title to Aquitaine.

Chiselers are always with us, and Law exhibits a half noble with a clipped rim. To discourage such illicit gold pilfering someone had the bright idea of edging coins with religious sentiments. Law shows a noble, intact, that may have been spared by its entreaty, in Latin, from the Sixth Psalm: "O Lord, rebuke me not in Thine anger."

(In other instances this pious strategy seems not to have helped. Words are missing from Charles I coins originally saying "I reign under the auspices of Christ" and "God protects His worshipers." Ultimately, a solution to the problem was reached with so-called "safeguards": circumambient mottoes that could not be removed without doing enough damage to render the coins unusable.)

Among the rarer coins in Law's, or anyone's, collection would be those from the reign of Edward V (April-June 1483). This Edward was one of the two young brothers imprisoned in the Tower of London by their uncle, Richard, Duke of Gloucester. Although history has never resolved the question, Richard is generally presumed to have had the children murdered on his way to becoming Richard III. Such was the view espoused by Shakespeare, and Law admits that, as the son of a Shakespeare professor, he subscribes to it. Considering its brevity, the number of coins issued during Edward's reign is necessarily limited. Only six are known to exist, one of which belongs to Law. This type of coin, called an angel and

The gold coins of Great Britain are particularly treasured as portraits in miniature of every monarch from Henry VIII to the reigning Queen Elizabeth.

continuing under other regimes, bears the image of an angel, in this case Michael, slaying a dragon. Ironically, the angel of Edward V's time carries the Duke of Gloucester's mark, a boar's head, indicating that he is Edward's protector.

In 1489 Henry VII struck a beautiful new coin of considerably greater value than any previously known: the sovereign. Its distinctive feature was a royal portrait. Law owns one of the first four surviving specimens.

The issuance of new sovereigns over the course of Henry VIII's reign provides a virtual portrait gallery featuring the king in the process of aging. Ultimately we arrive at the familiar likeness of the fat, older king with the beard. Certain coins also indicate changes in his marital status, some crowns being stamped with the initials H and K for Henry and Katharine of Aragon, others with H and A. After the A (Anne Boleyn), the monarch apparently decided not to go on recording replacements. During this period we get the first coins with lions and with creatures resembling unicorns. Law points out that the skill required to strike such sharply detailed designs with hand tools is astonishing.

So forceful was Henry's personality that for several years after his successor, Edward VI, superseded him on the coins, Henry's name remained. And the first images of Edward show him without a crown. The only child born to Henry's third wife, Jane Seymour, Edward was the apple of his father's eye but, as the portraits on the sovereigns indicate, did not resemble him. The last coins, depicting him in his teens, proclaim, "The hand of God will protect him." This prediction proved untrue: he died in 1553, just sixteen years old.

As might be expected, Elizabeth I, on the throne for 45 years, dominates an entire generation of coins, including highly valuable triple sovereigns. On one piece of par-

ticular rarity she is seen, like Edward III, aboard ship. Another in Law's collection captures her coiffure and dress in unusual and exquisite detail. As with her father, the passage of time is traceable in her features. The periods of James I, Charles I, Cromwell, Charles II, William and Mary, the Georges, and their successors come alive through distinctive coins, until finally we reach the Victorian threshold of our own era.

"Some people," says Law, "think the most beautiful British coin ever minted was one called Una and the Lion, honoring Victoria." This derives from Spenser's *Faerie Queene*, in which Una represents Truth and the lion attends and guards her. The lovely portrait of the queen as Una was struck in 1839 when she was a young woman.

Victoria had the longest reign in British history, from 1837 to 1901. A coin issued on the fiftieth anniversary of her reign shows her wearing a little cap. A later coin represents her in widowhood, with veil and double chin. Still later, the extra chin—perhaps by a wave of the royal wand—has vanished.

While there are beautiful coins from the reign of George V, none honors the next in line for the throne, Edward, since he chose to abdicate rather than be crowned as Edward VIII.

And so we come to the present day and Elizabeth II, who, through her place in the sequence of gold coins, partakes of the glamour of history—so easily lost when the latest in a royal procession is one's contemporary.

Given a collection made up of money, the question naturally arises as to its worth in the marketplace. Tom Law, who has assembled his with much care and obvious satisfaction, clearly has no immediate thought of disposing of it. He acknowledges, however, that if his collection were put up for sale, "I'd be disappointed if it didn't bring at least a million and a half."

Highest Price for an Ugly Work of Art

In 1986 Jerry J. Moore, a Houston shopping center magnate, parted with $6.5 million for a 1931 French-made Bugatti Royale Berline de Voyage. The price was the highest ever paid for an automobile. After the auction, Moore explained that he didn't "crave cars," though he had "respect and love for them," but, that as an investment, classic cars "will have done considerably better ten years from now than C.D.s, a savings account, or anything else."

Moore also went on record with the opinion that his shiny black-and-yellow Bugatti limousine was ugly— "but," he was quick to add, "a work of art." Certainly it is a vehicle of impressive presence, almost twenty feet long and weighing well over three tons. Originally priced at $45,000, it was once sold for $1,500 by its European owner, struggling to survive in World War II.

At the same auction in which Moore acquired the Bugatti, one of six of this model known to exist, he also bought three more classics. The first was a smaller and more elegant 1938 Bugatti four-door sedan, for $70,000. The other two were sporty Duesenbergs: a 1931 roadster ($800,000) and a 1933 "speedster" ($600,000). All four came under the auctioneer's hammer in Reno, Nevada, on the occasion of the final dismantling of a collection assembled over many years by the late gambling casino tycoon Bill Harrah. At one time Harrah had more than 1,400 automobiles, a kind of retrospective of practically every car ever made, along with some railroad rolling stock and an assortment of boats and airplanes.

Moore's collection consists of close to 270 cars, most of them antique Duesenbergs. He also has a group of special Mercedes from the 1930s and 22 twelve-cylinder Ferraris. For everyday good looks and utility he keeps a dozen new Rolls Royces around the house, the house being a 40-room chateau imported from France. He started buying cars, he says, because "when I was a kid I didn't have one." Born in Houston to Polish immigrant parents, he grew up lacking more than a car: on rainy days he sometimes went to school barefoot to save his shoes. A high school dropout, he spent a successful 12 years selling vacuum cleaners, then turned to low-cost housing construction, and from that to building shopping centers. His wife, Jean, and three grown children are associated with him in his business. Today his net worth is estimated at more than $700 million.

Moore's future building plans include a museum in Houston for his collection of classics.

Seven Bugatti Royales were built; six still exist. This one, from 1931, was Ettore Bugatti's personal car. It was bought at auction by Jerry J. Moore in 1986 for $6.5 million, the highest price ever paid for an automobile at that time. The body is all wood and was made using hundreds of small blocks and veneer panels to form the contours.

PERSONAL and PRIVATE

A Special Zest

Prodigal Texas has provided favorable conditions for collections on a grandiose scale. But someone like William F. Runyon, a pediatric dentist in Fort Worth, offers evidence that the taste and dedication needed to form a superior collection are not a prerogative of the super-rich. In a nice house in a nice residential section on a conventional-size plot of ground, Runyon has one of the most exciting collections around.

What accounts for its special flair? First of all, the collector's canny ability to distinguish between the meritorious and the meretricious in the current parade. He possesses a self-confidence that permits him to buy what he believes in, whether or not anyone else has approved, let alone seen it. Not that everything owned by William Runyon and his wife, Beverly, is the work of emerging artists. Established names are here, too. Some pieces are out of the past, their worth very likely recognized by the Runyons just before the world at large began to discover or rediscover them.

While Beverly Runyon and their six children share his pleasure in his acquisitions, the collecting impulse is definitely Bill's. As a 20-year-old visiting in Chicago, with no previous exposure to museums, he discovered the Art Institute and became an habitué. Neither then nor later did he have any schooling in art. He made his first purchase after completing his dental training and setting up practice in Fort Worth. With time he advanced far enough in knowledge and commitment to not only put together his own collection but to be elected president and subsequently chairman of the board of trustees of the Fort Worth Art Museum. This institution's focus, like Runyon's, is on work of the twentieth century.

Walking into the Runyons' living room, with the dining room opening invitingly just beyond, one has something to look at it in every direction. A quick eye catcher is a group consisting of teapot, cups, saucers, and dishes, all of similar fanciful design, painted in cheerful colors—blue, green, and lavender, with orange trim. One characteristic pattern features a tree with a sinuous black trunk and limbs from which hang bright balloon shapes. The ceramist, Clarice Cliff, now dead, worked in England in the '20s and '30s. Runyon had never heard of Cliff when he came across a book about her. Charmed by the photographs of the pottery, he began to search for it in London. Finally he

Prominent among William Runyon's collection of twentieth-century art is the vibrant work of English ceramist Clarice Cliff.

spotted a piece through a shop window; the proprietor of the shop was able to tell him where to find more, and thus that particular collection within a collection was begun.

Across the room is a furniture grouping: small rectangular table and two round-backed chairs, all in black lacquer. These were created by Josef Hoffmann around the turn of the century for the celebrated Fledermaus Cafe in Vienna, which he designed as well. Hoffmann was one of the animating spirits of the Secession movement of artists and architects who quit the conservative academy in Vienna to establish their own organization. Since the Runyons made their purchase, Vienna Secession has inspired museum exhibitions in Paris, New York, and Vienna itself.

Other furniture includes a graceful coffee table by the

sculptor-graphic artist Sol LeWitt; a larger glass-top and black tubular metal table by LeCorbusier and Mies' classic Barcelona chair. Good for a shock and a chuckle is a chair by Claire Dreyer, Adirondack style in cast aluminum, painted white, and crawling with real-looking black mice. Once the shock has worn off, it might be thought to have outlived its function. (One is put in mind of a Thomas Love Peacock novel where a character, showing a visitor through his elaborate garden with unconventional plantings and sudden twists and turns, explains that its purpose is to surprise. The guest asks, "But what about the second time around?") Maybe the mouse chair is justified by the fact that there is a first time for everyone who sees it.

John Duff, a sculptor, is represented by a primitive-

The sinuous tree shape and bright, cheerful colors are characteristic of Cliff's pottery, which was produced in England in the twenties and thirties.

looking work produced by a personally developed process: Duff first constructs a form out of plywood, paints the inside, then, before it is dry, lines it with fiberglass. He pulls the fiberglass out with layers of the paint and plywood clinging to it—and *voilà* a sculpture.

A tabletop sculpture by Rockne Krebs, a crystal prism on a marble base, sits on a small deco table before a window. Beautiful in itself, the prism refracts light throughout the rooms onto surrounding surfaces, during the day casting colors in shifting patterns as the sun's position changes.

Attached to a wall is a simple sculpture, *Brass Progressions* which, from a distance, could pass for an elegant lighting fixture. The artist is Donald Judd. Further examples of Judd's work are *Red Relief*, among his earliest sculptural pieces, and a later glass, Plexiglas, and steel-box construction which hangs in the master bedroom.

Runyon has a way of choosing works that are atypical of their creators. A five-panel screen by Jim Dine is decorated on both sides with abstract compositions. Ed Ruscha applies a mixture of pastel and gunpowder to unusual effect in a picture titled *Hollywood*. Helen Frankenthaler compresses her expansive, free-flowing line to small compass on a painted tile.

Delivering in more or less expected style are such stars as Lichtenstein, Warhol, Calder (with a watercolor), Stella, Rauschenberg, Rosenquist, Oldenberg (a drawing of the *Typewriter Eraser*), Donald Sultan, with two of his ubiquitous furry black lemons, Tom Wesselman, Nancy Graves, Alfred Jensen, Christopher Wilmarth, and Michael Lucero.

Texas artists have their innings, and most of them appear likely to become widely known. Remember the names of Jim Woodson, Patricia Tillman, Ron Tomlinson, Joe Guy, and Ed Blackburn. Blackburn's painting of Marilyn Monroe and Don Murray in a scene from *Bus Stop* has a special strength and poignancy.

Californians also figure prominently, among them Ed Keinholz, Tom Holland, Billy Al Bengston, Jerry McMillan, San Francis, Kenny Price, and Sam Richardson. The Richardson sculpture belonging to Runyon is a smaller version of a work commissioned for the Los Angeles Olympics.

A collection being formed as new place settings are completed is a dinner service crafted by Dorothy Hafner, a New Yorker. Though the overall effect is consistent in bold color and pattern, each individual piece is different from every other. The idea is to mix one's own to taste, and the Runyons have spent hours experimenting with various combinations. Once they've settled on what they particularly like together, they mark the pieces on the back for quick future assembly. Then a new shipment comes along, suggesting additional possibilities.

Displayed in an informal family room, the Hafner ware holds its own against the timeless artistry of Mimbres (New Mexico and Arizona Indian) pottery and Huisol Indian masks from Mexico. Also from Mexico, and New Mexico, are carved wooden animals. Throughout the house, new and old mingle congenially. Daughter Chelsea's bed, piled with bears, is brass, from around 1890—the fruit of a tireless search that took Runyon to the home, in Houston, of the South's leading dealer in brass beds (he'd been keeping this one off the market for himself). There are antique quilts—a choice few visible, the rest in storage. These along with pre-Columbian pottery, still much in evidence, were among the Runyons' earliest acquisitions.

And—oh, yes—over the years Runyon has collected stamps and coins.

In part to cope with the problem of dwindling space, and in part because Bill Runyon has a strong streak of the dealer, he has taken to selling art as well as buying it. For as long as he retains his interest in replacing what goes out, his collection may be counted on to rank with Texas' freshest and liveliest.

51

Meyer pottery from Bexar County, Texas, is a mainstay of Greer's personal collection and the subject of one of her books.

PERSONAL and PRIVATE

Collector as Researcher

A one-gallon pitcher from the San Antonio Pottery, circa 1930, is covered with a Bristol white glaze air brushed with cobalt.

Georgeanna Greer prefers to think of herself as a historical researcher rather than as a collector. Nevertheless, as a result of her research, she owns one of the finest collections anywhere of Texas pottery and American stoneware.

"Sometimes it's a bigger thrill," she says, "to find an old pottery site than a piece of old pottery." From shards picked up at an abandoned factory it may be possible to deduce certain facts: for example, the kind of kiln the potters used, the types of ware they turned out, and where their clay came from. Information also may be gleaned regarding the way people lived: what they ate and how they served and preserved it, how they beautified their surroundings, and much more. Thanks in no small part to the scholarly zeal of Dr. Greer, a San Antonio pediatrician, the store of such information has been steadily growing.

In childhood she had been captivated by a beautiful set of doll dishes belonging to her grandmother. When her family spent two years in Arizona, she collected miniature Indian pots. During subsequent travels to Mexico she added pitchers, still on the dimunitive scale of her grandmother's doll china.

The year 1943 was an important one for Greer: she received her M.D. degree from the University of Texas Medical School in Galveston and married a fellow graduate, a future thoracic surgeon, Dr. Sam Greer. The couple moved to Michigan, where both served their internships. While in Ann Arbor she took a night course in pottery making.

She studied the craft at a more sophisticated level at the McNay Art Institute in San Antonio beginning in 1957, after she and her husband had moved permanently to that city. They now had three children, and even working only part time at medicine, Georgeanna Greer was busy; but she managed to pursue her interest in ceramics. Her instructors during ten years at the McNay included such major talents as Harding Black, George Palovich, and Ishmael Soto.

The more she learned about various techniques and the many differences in clays, glazes, and other materials, the more Greer realized how little she—or anyone—knew about the early pottery of Central Texas. Buying clay one day in Seguin, which is surrounded by rich deposits, she was shown some shards from a pottery that once had operated in the neighborhood. She went to look for more on

her own, but at that time found nothing; the spark, however, had been struck. She began to visit abandoned pottery sites or currently active potteries and acquainted herself with what was in museums. Also, she reviewed census records as a way of learning who the Texas potters were from 1850 on.

Before this ambitious project got fully under way, a serious blood disease put Greer out of commission. Her illness lasted four years—years of enforced idleness and depression. Then, as mysteriously as it had started, the condition cleared up and she was able to resume her research.

With increasing knowledge came an ever-wider curiosity. To become better informed about salt glazes, which European potters introduced to the American colonies before 1800, she undertook research abroad. Recently she has been working as a consultant with the University of South Carolina on a study of southern alkaline glazes. Originally, such glazes were achieved by mixing wood ash and clay; in the late nineteenth century they were altered by the addition of various fluxes, including ground glass or lime.

Much of what Greer has learned has gone into two books, *American Stoneware* and *The Meyer Family, Mas-*

ter Potters of Texas. The latter, written in collaboration with her teacher, Harding Black, grew out of an exhibition she had organized at San Antonio's Witte Museum. Meyer pottery is a mainstay of Greer's personal collection; she has some 400 pieces.

The Meyer Pottery was established in 1887 near Atascosa by two German immigrants, J.F.W. (William) Meyer and Franz Shultz, who had met en route to Texas two years earlier. Meyer married Schultz's daughter and fathered two sons, who both joined the family business. The pottery remained operative until 1964 when the surviving son, then 75, retired.

What makes Meyer glazed pottery especially appealing to collectors, according to Greer, is its color, which runs through innumerable subtle gradations from brown to mustard green. This particular range relates to the slip clay—clay used for coating or decoration—dug from a small hill on the bank of Leon Creek, an area contained today within the boundaries of Kelly Field in San Antonio.

Churns were a popular Meyer product. So were jugs, jars, baking dishes, bowls, pitchers, spittoons, ant traps, chamber pots, cookie jars, poultry fountains, water coolers, flower pots, and other florists' ware. Meyer jug handles were attached in unusual fashion, to the shoulders of pots rather than to their mouth rings. Also, many of the handle ends were applied in a distinctive way, the clay being cut off in a sharp wedge shape, then joined to the wall of the pot with the pressure of a finger, leaving a fingerprint.

Some articles were turned out with special features. A very early one-gallon jug, for example, carries the legend made by an impressed metal stamp: "WILLIAM RADAM'S MICROBE KILLER." Radam was a horticulturist who ran a small seed and garden store in Austin. Convinced that all illnesses and diseases, including cancer, were caused by the multiplication of microbes, he developed a patent medicine that he believed—or claimed to believe—meant death for microbes and could cure practically anything. It might either be taken internally or rubbed on the skin. Within two years of running his first ad in the *Austin Statesman* on August 30, 1887, Radam had 18 factories producing his panacea and was living in style on New York's Fifth Avenue.

Meyer salesmen traveled with sample kits of miniatures, and Greer owns a number of these scaled-down prototypes. Thus her collecting has come full circle, leading her back to the tiny Indian pots that were the first things she bought.

Greer acknowledges that she thinks of herself as a researcher first and collector second because there isn't much of top quality left to collect. Though she doesn't say so, her own successful efforts to rescue the best stonewares of old Texas and the old South from undeserved neglect have had a lot to do with their present popularity—hence scarcity and costliness.

The yellow patterning on a three-gallon churn from Bexar County, circa 1880, was caused by contact with fire and wood ash during the firing.

PERSONAL and PRIVATE

Toys Step off the Page

Popeye, the sailor man, is Jim McNabb's favorite cartoon character.

Houston's climate as much as anything else is responsible for turning Jim McNabb into a collector of comic-strip and comic-book toys. As a kid who grew up on Popeye and other mythic figures of Cartoonland, he accumulated comic books by the carload. As an adult with a college degree in art and with landscape design as a profession, McNabb continued to value these childhood treasures, but with a deeper appreciation of their artistic skill. Eventually, however, he had to face the fact that "when you live in Houston and have 95-percent humidity all the time," piles of paper simply aren't practical. They retain moisture and attract roaches. So around 1970 McNabb switched over to collecting his cartoon characters in the form of toys, along with replicas of objects associated with them. In addition to a number of Buck Rogers figures, for example, he has a Buck Rogers bomb sight, chemical lab, fireworks set (with a cannon that shoots off a firecracker), pistols, holsters, and a Buck Rogers game and puzzle.

Joe Palooka, Moon Mullins, Captain Marvel, Howdy Doody, and Superman, among many others, are surrounded by the clothing, gadgetry, and appurtenances—such as Joe's boxing gloves—familiar to their devotees. An entire cabinet is given over to Popeye likenesses—stationary or windup—and articles (e.g., cans of spinach) related to the feisty sailor man. His unique physique and physiognomy turn up on lamps, penny banks, ashtrays, and battery-operated toys. Popeye, incidentally, is McNabb's favorite character.

Disney icons from Mickey Mouse to the Seven Dwarfs and beyond are much in evidence in McNabb's house. Blondie and Dagwood, Mortimer Snerd, and Felix the Cat are other old friends. McNabb is too young to have shared in the worldwide adulation of Charlie Chaplin at the height of his popularity, nor was he around in the '20s when the Toonerville Trolley That Meets All the Trains was jingling and jangling its bumpy way across the nation's newspapers; but he has Chaplin figurines, diminutive bowler hats and canes, and a so-called Crackerjack version of the trolley. Little hands used to rummage eagerly for toys in the Crackerjack confectionery boxes. McNabb's Toonerville Trolley happens not to have come from such a box but resembles other small, cheap items that did and of which he has a representative assortment.

It is a source of considerable pride to McNabb that his

McNabb's cartoon-land collection, in scope and variety, is the most complete of its kind in Texas.

collection, in scope and variety, is the most complete of its kind in the state of Texas.

Asked if he ever plays with his toys, McNabb says no and adds that he doesn't allow his daughter or her friends to lay hands on them either. Not that the kids are deprived; they have plenty of less precious playthings to keep them happily occupied.

Though the collection has grown quite valuable, a circumstance about which its owner has mixed feelings, he tends not to dwell on the possibility of theft. "People say, 'Don't you worry about somebody stealing that stuff?' I say, 'What could they do with it?' Sure, they could take it somewhere and sell it, but when people break in they want cameras, they want coins—something they can take to the nearest pawn shop. I had someone break in here one time and they took cameras and TV sets."

On the one hand, McNabb is gratified that the collection is worth more than was spent on it, while on the other he hates to see speculators taking advantage of the current craze for nostalgia. "Right now," he says, "anything from people's childhood—bubblegum cards to dolls—is as hot as can be. Everyone in the world seems to be getting into it and prices are going crazy."

One undesirable side effect is that McNabb finds himself having to keep an eye out for crooks. He occasionally sells toys, not to make money but to be able to buy others and fill in gaps in his collection. His contact with the purchaser is usually by phone. "I used to say when they bought something, 'I'll send it out to you tomorrow,' and they'd say, 'You don't want to wait for a check?' I'd say, 'Are you going to rip me off for some crazy toy?'" McNabb tells of receiving a beautifully typed letter from a man in Milwaukee asking to see lists, then a second letter requesting certain photographs. McNabb obliged both times, then mailed off the toys chosen. Two months later, not having been paid, he called the phone number on the letterhead and found it was nonexistent.

In another instance he had to make a trip to Denver to collect what was owed him. Now he is more cautious in his dealings with strangers.

At first blush it would seem that nothing could be less likely to contain anything controversial than a houseful of toys. McNabb has examples of some old toys, however, that are deplored by members of the black community. One, a wind-up, depicts a black man trying to make off with a stolen chicken while a dog hangs by its teeth to his torn pants leg.

McNabb defends the inclusion of this in his collection on the ground that, while he deplores its implicit racism, it is typical of many toys made early in the century and as such is a part of the historical record. Somewhat offsetting the effect of this toy is a little figure of Louis Armstrong, trumpet to lips, cheeks bulging as he produces the notes beloved of jazz aficionados. Unfortunately, any accompanying sound has to be in the viewer's head. But then, it's the function of toys to free the imagination, and, as Keats pointed out, unheard melodies *are* sweeter.

The mythic figures of childhood comic books populate McNabb's Houston house.

The Return
of King William

Within the restored 1876 Italianate limestone mansion in San Antonio's oldest historic district is housed a treasure trove of the multifaceted collections of Walter Nold Mathis.

Walter Nold Mathis occupies a special niche among Texas collectors. His house in San Antonio's King William district is a cornucopia of collections. Though richly varied, they all reflect a concern with history, some of it local history in which successive generations of his family have taken part.

The house itself is historic, having been built in 1876 in opulent Italianate style by German stonemasons for a well-to-do hardware merchant, not a Mathis ancestor. About 15 years later a three-story tower was added. The city in those days was enjoying a prosperity enhanced by the arrival of the new railroad; but by 1967 when Mathis bought the old limestone mansion on King William Street, it was a rundown building in a virtual slum.

The neighborhood's subsequent resurgence owes a good deal to Mathis' initiative and effort. Originally—in the early 1700s—the acreage belonged to the Spanish mission that later became known as the Alamo, and served as farmland. When German immigrants moved in, in the mid-1800s, they called the community's main street Kaiser Wilhelm after their first monarch to bear that name. The houses they built for themselves and others varied in type and degree of elegance, from the Italian-style villa of the hardware merchant to cottages, gingerbread Victorian, and Greek Revival. With Germany as arch-enemy in World War I, Kaiser Wilhelm Street underwent a change of identity to the more acceptable King William Street. In the late 1920s, in the aftermath of severe flooding by the San Antonio River, many residents abandoned the district. That marked the beginning of its downfall. World War II with its housing shortage hastened it: many of the already-deteriorated structures were converted into rooming houses. The first sign of a turnaround occurred when one of the old mansions was rehabilitated to serve as headquarters for the San Antonio Conservation Society. Mathis was active in raising money for this project, and when, a couple of years later, he was driven from his own residence by construction of a freeway, he thought of the King William district as a haven.

Since no one else was buying property there, he had free choice; and having selected one of the handsomest houses, set on ample grounds, he proceeded to tear it apart, eliminate rooms that had been created for multiple occupancy, clean, repair, refurbish, and reestablish the garden. Not

*Mathis' collections of objects
and furnishings, some inherited,
some purchased, are assimilated
into the everyday life of the
house, such as the Napoleonic
articles in the drawing room.*

After Mathis restored his Villa Finale, he bought 14 other dilapidated houses in
the tiny enclave known as King William, originally settled by prosperous German
immigrants.

wanting to live in solitary splendor, he bought 14 other King William houses for reclamation, thus paving the way for a real estate boom and designation of the whole area as a small historic district. To his own house he gave the name Villa Finale, because, he explains, "I have no intention of ever moving again."

Mathis, a bachelor, is a thrice-decorated World War II bomber pilot. A hearty man, over six feet tall, he is a vice president of Shearson Lehman/American Express and a lavish host in his showplace home. As a child he read everything he could find about Napoleon; this persisting preoccupation has given rise to an outstanding collection. There are prints on the walls relating to the Little Corporal; there are bronze busts of him as a general and as first consul; ivory triptychs of him and his second wife, Marie Louise; other portrait figures in bronze, silver, and wood, one atop a clock; a miniature replica of his casket, bronze and gold; plumed helmets, swords, intaglio medallions of the period and a late-nineteenth-century copy of a washstand used by Empress Josephine at Malmaison.

Interest in things military spills over into other objects, some from Texas' own past: Currier and Ives lithographs of the Mexican War, Staffordshire ware of a Texian Campaigne series depicting cavalry charges, gilt-and-bronze candelabras in the likeness of Indian warriors, and Bowie knives. Mathis' grandfather, Sam Bell, was a silversmith in town, and the centerpiece of his descendant's Bowie knife collection is one by Bell. He also has a silver coin collection including some pieces made by Bell, the earliest dated 1852. Silver in other forms—goblets, pitchers, epergnes, tea services, and such—constitutes a collateral collection. There is in addition a collection of American, English, and Continental pewter.

The Onderdonks, Robert J. and Julian, father and son, are painters prized in Texas. Robert specialized in historical subjects such as *The Fall of the Alamo,* executed in 1903. Julian introduced the "bluebonnet school," a style of bucolic painting that still has devoted practitioners. Mathis owns 30 Onderdonks.

A small but choice collection of icons includes ones of Spanish, Spanish colonial, Greek, and Russian origin. Snuff boxes have been collected from all parts of the world wherever the practice of inhaling finely pulverized tobacco has taken hold.

Much more than Bell's handiwork has come to Mathis by way of ancestors: furniture, quilts, and crystal, for example. To these family possessions have been added complementary pieces, so that collections have formed naturally around heirlooms. This is the case in respect to early Texas furniture and pottery. A sitting room, bedrooms, and other informal parts of the house contain a mix of antiques, some inherited, some acquired from outside sources. In a basement recreation room, nineteenth-century poker and domino tables—the former from the Kendall Inn in Boerne, Texas, the latter from a tavern in New Braunfels—are flanked by captain's chairs from the Old San Antonio Casino Club. A collection of beer mugs from San Antonio's Pearl Brewery contributes to the room's relaxed, good-old-days ambiance.

It is a particular charm of the Mathis collections that the objects are not set apart from the life of the house. There is nothing of the exhibit about them. Those that have practical application are put to use. All help create the feeling of past-in-present and present-in-past, offering a sense of continuity that gives meaning to tradition and lends zest to day-to-day existence.

PERSONAL and PRIVATE

Edging into Rare Books

Fore-edge paintings were done by wandering artists in exchange for lodging.

Dr. Charles Tandy, a Dallas anesthesiologist, recalls his first sight of the *Nuremberg Chronicles*. A copy was shown him by Decherd Turner, at that time librarian of the Bridwell (theological) Library at Southern Methodist University in Dallas.

The *Chronicles*, says Tandy, "is one of the most interesting fifteenth-century books around. It was the first profusely illustrated book, with more than 1,700 illustrations. The subject is the history of the world from the beginning to July 23, 1493. The day I saw it for the first time I never dreamed I'd have one. Now I have three."

One is in Latin, the language of the original publication. The other two are in German, the native tongue of the scholar-compiler, Hartmann Schedel. So popular was this work that it was widely pirated by spiritual ancestors of those publishers who operate today outside the copyright law. One of Tandy's German versions is a pirated edition.

The doctor edged into collecting old and rare books in the process of closing certain gaps in his education. Until becoming accredited in his medical specialty, he had concentrated almost entirely on learning what he needed to know to become a doctor. A native of Abilene, he graduated from that city's Hardin-Simmons University, then went through Southwestern Medical School in Dallas. It struck him after earning his degree that he had had to be so single-minded in his studies that whole areas of literature, history, and art were unfamiliar territory. Starting from what *was* familiar, he began to look into the background of anesthesia. It would be interesting, he thought, to pick up some history that way, even though the history did not go back very far. Prior to the 1840s, getting a patient drunk was about the best a surgeon could do to relieve pain.

Delving into original sources, including grisly accounts of operations before anesthesia, Tandy found himself reading—and buying—old books. One of his acquisitions dates from 1601: the first English translation of notes made by the naturalist Pliny the Elder, whose observations on curatives derived from plants and animals are among the earliest surviving writings along such lines. Scientific and medical discoveries of the eighteenth and nineteenth centuries also are represented in Tandy's books and pamphlets from the pens of the discoverers.

In the course of pursuing his hobby, Tandy made the acquaintance of others who prized old books, and many of these people became friends. His collecting interests broadened to include books on a variety of subjects, but a special chord was struck when Tandy saw a fellow bibliophile's early seventeenth-century Bible printed in London by Robert Barker. This happened to be one of Barker's so-called "Wicked Bibles," loosed on the public as a result of a malicious trick. Barker had the Bible market sewn up at the time, being the only person with a royal license to print copies of the Good Book. Understandably, other printers were resentful, and one of them surreptitiously tinkered with the type for the Seventh Commandment, changing adultery from proscribed to approved behavior. Many of these Bibles came out before the mischief was noticed.

Tandy, too, began to collect Bibles. An original King James Bible (1611) is among his treasures, along with an even earlier one, a 1541 Great Bible from the reign of Henry VIII. A previous owner who obviously disliked the monarch, and probably his illustrated Bible as well, had scratched out Henry's face in a woodcut.

These days Tandy has less time for his books than he did while building up the collection; both he and his wife have become increasingly involved in Dallas civic affairs. But the thought of selling any of them—even at a considerable profit—never crosses his mind. "They're part of me," he says.

Dallas anesthesiologist Charles Tandy began his rare book collection by delving into the origins of his own medical specialty. Later, he also began to collect Bibles, such as the side-latched King James version, circa 1611.

PERSONAL and PRIVATE

Memories of the Sixties

On the long private drive from the public road in North Dallas to Lupe Murchison's house, the visitor is greeted by signs posted at intervals on the lawn: "You are under surveillance." "Proceed no farther." "Beware—vicious dogs." "You are in our gun sights." If those are not the exact words, they pretty much convey the message. The proper visitor is happy to have phoned ahead and know he is expected.

There are other things to catch the eye during the approach, examples of the landscape architect's and sculptor's art. Notable among the latter is a broad aluminum ribbon extending many yards along one side of the driveway. The ribbon does not lie flat: it has been shaped by Benni Efrat, an Israeli sculptor, into a repetitive pattern of loops, with a cube set between each pair of loops, seemingly holding the ribbon to the ground. One with a memory of Angkor in Cambodia may have the sense of seeing an abstract version of the rows of almost identical imposing, seated figures which line the avenue leading to the temple known as Angkor Thom.

Closer to the house are other sculptures, including a camel-humped bronze, *Taxidermy 4*, by Nancy Graves. One is shortly to learn that this is the second incarnation of the same work bought by the Murchisons. They commissioned the first, which was executed in wax. After setting it up indoors, the owners took off on a trip. By the time they returned, all that was left of their camel—perhaps installed before too sunny a window—was a pile of melted wax on the floor. Graves, asked to duplicate her creation, did so in a more permanent medium.

The house is an ideal place to display art, being of generous dimensions with beautifully proportioned, light rooms, wide halls, and an ample foyer. It was built nearly half a century ago "out in the country" by Clint Murchison, Sr., on the former site of the Dallas Polo Club. The country by now has moved much farther out, and there are busy highways, other houses, and commercial structures near by, but this mansion is surrounded by sufficient acreage to retain its air of isolation. When Clint Murchison's children were grown and parenting children of their own, he and son John swapped houses.

Lupe Murchison, John's widow, recalls that when her children were of school age they were embarrassed to bring their friends home. She and John had started in the

Standing Girl, *a Frank Gallo sculpture, stands in the entry against a pair of Charles Aberg oils.*

Snaking its way across the expansive grounds that lead to the Lupe Murchison house in Dallas is an undulating aluminum sculpture by Israeli artist Benni Efrat.

An antique French dining table is topped with a mirrored surface to reflect the Sheffield candelabrum and hand-painted Japanese panels.

1960s to collect the art of the period and kids, ever conservative, especially where Mom and Dad are concerned, considered much of it embarrassing. Friends of the adult Murchisons also regarded the art as outré, unsuited to a conventional if more than ordinarily spacious and elegant residence.

In the 1980s the Murchison art has lost its initial shock value and no longer seems out of place. Some of it, such as certain kinetic works (e.g., one in which colored disks roll back and forth on tracks that shift up and down in a glass case), have an almost old-fashioned charm. Most of the other pieces have attained a kind of maturity, quietly—or in some instances loudly—asserting their claim to be taken seriously after their novelty has waned.

When the Murchisons were just starting to acquire, new names on the art scene included Helen Frankenthaler, Kenneth Noland, Robert Rauschenberg, Louise Nevelson, and Robert Motherwell. These are still in evidence in the collection, along with Ernest Trova, Esteban Vicente, Morris Louis, Claes Oldenberg, Mac Whitney, Robert Graham, Frank Stella, George Ortman, George Rickey, Jim Dine, and others, some celebrated, some less well known. The house, remodeled and added on to, easily accommodates a diversity of styles.

A note of levity and, for theater lovers, of nostalgia is introduced into this collection by the presence of a giant rabbit. Meet the original Harvey of Mary Chase's celebrated, long-run Broadway play. Harvey appears to be made out of papier-mâché.

Because the Murchisons accumulated much more than can be displayed at any one time, a little house near the main one, former servants' quarters, provides storage space for the overflow. From time to time works are rotated; the eye is refreshed, the collection kept alive.

A Helen Frankenthaler oil and a bronze sculpture by Alberto Viani entitled Nude Seducto *are displayed in the marble-paved stairwell.*

Thoughts for Food

Dallas artist Pam Nelson makes no secret of the fact that she likes food. Much of her work, sculpturesque or using various materials at hand such as cloth and beads, is based on fruits, vegetables, meat, and potatoes. "Food," she says, perhaps with tongue partly in cheek, "is the only art form that changes people physically."

As a collector she tends to favor the same sorts of creations that emerge from her own studio. Her acquisitions are by no means limited, however, to representations of the edible.

The comfortable, casually furnished house Nelson shares with two teenaged sons, Keith and Charlie, and husband, Bill, evinces a sense of humor in the objects on display. That bunch of grapes, for instance: fabric-covered bottle caps. The crocheted cheese sandwich. Plastic artichokes. A plate of vinyl luncheon meats.

Or how about watercolors of TV dinners, baloney slices as cabinet knobs, a giant styrofoam ham atop the refrigerator? To say nothing of ice cream cones in silver candelabra and a bowl of sequined fruit.

In what has become a Christmas tradition, each family member gives Pam something he has made. She points to a hamburger with the trimmings, a serving of fish and chips, a Chinese dinner, and a waffle-and-eggs breakfast. A friend made her a birthday cake of cement.

Japanese restaurants often illustrate items on the menu with vinyl likenesses in the window. Nelson, who has some of these, criticizes the best of them as "almost too good." She explains, "I like things that are *really* fake!" Her collection includes examples of the latter, manufactured in Japan though showing Western influences. These can come out looking like little *trompe l'oeil* sculptures. One is a carton, tilted, from which milk appears to be pouring into a glass. The stream of milk, attached at the bottom to the glass, holds up the carton at the top.

Things-made-of-other-things are Nelson collectibles. Some simulate food, others do not. A handsome basket has been crocheted from bread wrappers. Braided cigar wrappers are shaped into a purse with the texture of reptile skin. Bubble gum is reincarnated as baloney. Note pads between two sponges, bonded together and painted, come out resembling a sandwich. Nelson likes to leave the price stickers on such novelties as a matter of historical record. It is the nature of the novelty business that the product

Dallas artist Pam Nelson became so absorbed in collecting examples of fake food that she began incorporating the ideas into her own artistic outlay, such as the ceramic Mexican food combination platter in the foreground.

keeps changing; these sandwiches, she says, will never be made again, and some day it may be of interest that they sold for three dollars.

Bottle caps can be put to a surprising number of uses, undergoing transformation to the point of being unrecognizable. A bottlecap ashtray and bottlecap urn belie their origins. So does a crucifix constructed of safety pins with beads slipped over the pins' shafts.

Perhaps the rarest pieces in the collection are carrots and a slice of apple pie, in plaster. They have little hooks so they can be hung up. A WPA artist during the depression made them to illustrate a lecture for school kids on nutrition.

Nelson does not spend time wondering whether what she collects is art. Some of the pieces may be simply decorative and amusing, like the earrings made out of plastic sushi. Some, in her view, qualify as folk art. Some, having been made by prison inmates, appeal to her as much on grounds of human interest as for any other reason.

One way in which Nelson's collecting differs from anyone else's is how she handles the situation if she wants to add something and can't find it. "I looked and looked for an enchilada dinner," she says. "Nobody was making them. So I made my own."

PERSONAL and PRIVATE

On from Midland

Geography is the answer given by Dallas real estate investor Alan M. May when asked how he and his wife, Marcia, happened to start collecting. The Mays own an idiosyncratic selection of contemporary art and some rare and unusual books. They also have a remarkable art reference library containing, among other things, approximately 4,000 *catalogues raisonnés*, those volumes, often generously illustrated, in which artists' careers are traced through a systematic record of their works.

"Twenty years ago," May explains, "we lived in Midland, Texas. It was easier to buy catalogues and study them on a quiet evening than to see fine art. By the time we moved to Dallas five years later we had the start of our library." It was then, too, that they began seriously acquiring paintings, drawings, and sculpture. Their chief interest has been in young, emerging artists, and their method is to continue buying from artists as their careers develop.

This has led to some intimate friendships. Jean-Michel Basquiat, who seeks to capture New York's gritty energy on graffiti-like canvases, accepted an invitation to be the Mays' guest when a primitivism show in which he was interested opened at the Dallas Museum of Art. The couple keep a spare apartment next to theirs and planned to put Basquiat up for a day or two. He started painting and stayed three weeks, reveling in the fact that no one had a phone number for him and he could get a lot of work

done. When he finally left, it was thanks to an appointment the Mays had set up for him in Paris to work with Picasso's printer.

"Then we took off for our place in Italy," says May, adding, "He showed up there and stayed a week."

May describes the kind of art they collect as mostly "lyrical surrealism." Some of the names whose works are on view in their home are Joseph Cornell, the Czech Jiri Kolar, a California student of the late Clifford Styll known as Jess, Julian Schnabel, Alfred Jensen, the young Scottish painter Stephen Campbell, British sculptor Julian Opie, and Texas painter Vernon Fisher. Of the outsized Campbell canvas dominating a wall of the living room, May says, "We had to wait a year to get something that small. His usual canvases are about ten feet tall, and taller."

Kolar's creations give a special sophisticated pleasure. They are sculptural, of a size to stand on shelves or table tops, constructed with applications of paper, rather in the manner of papier-mâché. The pattern or printing on the paper generally means something in terms of Kolar's theme. For example, he has made a Noah's ark, peopling it with every kind of creature, and working with paper from a Larousse Encyclopedia, which, because it encompasses practically everything that is known, signifies the universe.

Apart from the *catalogues raisonnés*, the Mays' book collection is strong in French nineteenth-century art, the old masters, and contemporary art. Probably the most precious, and certainly one of the most fascinating books, is titled *Scriptorium Florentinum*. This was published in an edition of 21 copies by a friend of the Mays whose family has had a textile business in Florence for five centuries. The book is a virtual history of the Renaissance told through correspondence of such figures as the Medicis, Michelangelo, and Machiavelli. Their letters have been reproduced on paper preserved from the period, each sheet then being tipped into the book.

In his anecdotal guided tour of the Dallas apartment, May mentions casually that they have an apartment in New York containing "a lot of contemporary stuff." They also, it appears, have a villa in Florence. Clearly, Alan and Marcia May have come a considerable distance since they had to satisfy their art hunger with *catalogues raisonnés* in Midland.

Spurs: Sexy . . . Sexist?

As far as he knows, Dwight W. Huber of Amarillo is the only collector specializing in a particular type of spur called gal-leg—or, sometimes in more refined parlance, lady's-leg.

Under either name, the spur in question has twin shanks shaped to resemble women's legs. At the end of each foot, positioned where it would be on conventional, non-anthropomorphic spurs, is a rowel—the sharp-toothed wheel that goads the rider's horse. While not all women may approve of the style introduced to the West in the late 1880s (the spread legs tend to be quite saucy looking, even brazen), it provides Huber with the basis for his unique and surprisingly varied collection. In addition to popular models of the gal-leg first produced in quantity by a certain J. R. McChesney, then by his contemporaries and by spur makers today, many were made to order to satisfy individual tastes. Decorative embellishments are imaginative and diverse. The legs offer room for motifs such as lilies, leaves, hearts, even peanuts. One cowboy had playing cards and dice worked into the design. A particularly rich-looking pair has a silver overlay on the legs inlaid with copper maple leaves in the heel band. Some of the ladies' slippers—and garters—are of gold or silver. Other parts of the spurs besides the extremities may be ornamented with special markings such as diamond-shaped arm-and-hammer symbols, perhaps representing a certain ranch, or with buttons made from Mexican pesos.

Huber's collection consists of 85 pairs of gal-legs. In a *Spur Collectors' Quarterly* he publishes, he has written:

"Despite the fact that almost every major and minor maker of hand-forged spurs built gal-legs, McChesney remains the acknowledged master of the type. The variations he crafted on the basic theme were apparently endless. . . . As a result, the chances of documenting every variety are almost nil; the chances of discovering new variations, on the other hand, are very good."

By an ironic twist, the technological enemy of the horse, the automobile, has made a contribution to spur manufacture. Melted-down Model T or Model A Ford axles have given the makers of spurs the finest-tempered metal they have ever worked with. As a consequence, collectors pay a premium for spurs containing this prized metal.

The same free-ranging imagination that goes into the design of the handsomest, and in some instances the wittiest, spurs can produce overly ornate specimens. A few in Huber's collection are garish, almost grotesque—interesting as examples of a whimsical idea pushed too far.

In the early 1950s, spurs and other riding gear and appurtenances were put up for auction at the Hearst estate, San Simeon, in southern California. Huber bought the entire spur collection, including pairs that had belonged to Tom Mix and other early Western movie stars. (One tall-in-the-saddle hero wore fourteen-karat gold-and-sterling-silver spurs characterized tersely by Huber as "overloaded.") He also acquired other Mix items but subsequently sold Mix's spurs.

While gal-legs are Huber's specialty, he and his wife, Terry, collect in other, unrelated areas. Their house is filled with unusual pieces of furniture including a Shaker settee with matching chairs, an antique Texas county courthouse desk and a handsome table and chairs from a Mexican barroom, the chairs emblazoned on their backs with beer ads. Colonial Mexican primitive religious paintings are another shared interest. Both Hubers enjoy traveling with collecting in mind as a refreshing change from their careers as teachers of English literature and composition at the local community college.

In recognition of the time and effort he has devoted to spurs, Huber has been the recipient of several pairs commissioned in his honor. Asked if he put them to practical use, he replied, "Well, no. Actually, I've never been on a horse!"

Two Loves

Although at first glance they seem to have nothing in common, Michael Carey's two collections share an important basic characteristic: every object makes a simple, direct esthetic statement.

One of the collections consists of Mexican folk art; the other comprises early twentieth-century furniture, lamps, and lighting fixtures. They blend very well in Carey's home in Austin, the polychromatic ebullience of the naive art providing cheerful contrast to the puritan plainness of chairs and tables by Gustav Stickley.

Carey, who has turned his preoccupation with a period and style of furnishing into a profession, sells Stickley and the decorative accessories that go with it from shops in both Austin and Manhattan's trendy SoHo. The loft he lives in while in New York contains more of the same, along with a supplementary collection of the folk art.

Gustav Stickley, originally Gustave (he simplified his name while eliminating the nonessential from his furniture design), died disheartened and forgotten in 1942. Earlier, he had been one of the country's leading tastemakers and a successful manufacturer and merchandiser. His story is the all-too-familiar one of the fine artist or craftsman (and Stickley was both) finding favor, and then—through no fault of his own—losing it, only to regain it after death.

Born in 1857 in Osceola, Wisconsin, Stickley was the oldest of six brothers. Trained by his father as a stonemason, he went to work as a young man for an uncle in Brandt, Pennsylvania, who made chairs. At age 41, still in the furniture business, he bought out a partner and established the Gustave Stickley Company in Eastwood, New York, a suburb of Syracuse. That same year, 1898, he traveled to Europe where he met, among others who were to influence him, an English architect and designer, Charles Voysey. Voysey himself showed the influence of William Morris, who in turn was indebted for some of his ideas to John Ruskin. Morris had set himself the mission of reviving the flagging decorative arts in England and making well-designed fabric, wall paper, rugs, and furniture available to the general public. ("What business have we with art at all," he asked, "unless we can share it?") Unfortunately, manufacturing costs were such that only the well-to-do could afford what Morris turned out.

Still, Stickley responded wholeheartedly to Morris' philosophy and to Voysey's lighter adaptation of Morris'

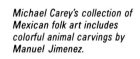

Michael Carey's collection of Mexican folk art includes colorful animal carvings by Manuel Jimenez.

Manhattan antiques dealer Michael Carey melds a collection of contrasts into a personal, direct aesthetic statement at his second home in Austin: the puritan plainness of Gustave Stickley's furniture with the ebullience of Mexican folk art. Complementing the furniture, and also produced in the first decade of the twentieth century, are the ceiling fixtures and table lamps. The wooden animals aligned just below ceiling level are by Manuel Jimenez. Candelario Medrano made the red rooster, also the ship and tower-like apartment building near the glass doors. Michael Tracy of San Ygnacio, Texas, executed the triptych painting on the far wall in 1981.

designs, and upon his return home he set a new course for himself. Previously his furniture had borrowed from historical models. Now he broke with the past and made squared-off, clean-lined pieces, counting on fine wood and meticulous workmanship to compensate for the absence of embellishment.

Showing off a table and some chairs today, Michael Carey explains, "It's all white oak, but it's all different. It differs in hardness, and in how the grains are closed or open. Some oaks are harder than others. Stickley used better wood than any of his competitors.

"At first he had a small company," Carey continues. "He would introduce something, make it for a year or two, then discontinue it. Those pieces are now rare."

As the public took to Stickley's Craftsman line, he started a magazine, *The Craftsman*. His aim, as he stated in the first issue, was "to substitute the luxury of taste for the luxury of costliness; to teach that beauty does not imply elaboration or ornament; to employ only those forms or materials which make for simplicity, individuality and dignity of effect."

People in great numbers subscribed to this credo and bought the furniture. They liked the slatted chair backs and the exposed dovetails and dowels that revealed the construction; they found the canvas or leather upholstery comfortable and practical. The overall sturdiness was appealing. The Stickley executive division moved from upstate New York to New York City and expanded business operations, allocating Craftsman franchises from one end of the country to the other. Gustav Stickley began building a housing development and a model farm in nearby New Jersey. In Manhattan he bought a bigger building with increased office space and showrooms and even opened a restaurant on the ground floor.

As so often happens, the expansion was ill-timed, based on a misreading of the situation. It was 1913, a year in which a new trend in decorating, spearheaded by Elsie de Wolfe, was fast gathering momentum. A large part of the public was ready to turn from the simple back to the fancy. The Arts and Crafts Movement, for which *The Craftsman* provided a forum, was losing its supremacy. In 1915 Stickley, disillusioned by what he saw as the failure of his efforts at education, was forced into bankruptcy. He never made a comeback in his own lifetime.

Carey's introduction to the folk art of Mexico came at San Antonio's Hemisfair in 1968 where collector Alexander Girard had mounted an exhibit. For his first acquisitions Carey started at the top, purchasing three terra-cotta dolls made by one of the leading contemporary Mexican workers in clay, Teodora Blanco. He has continued to acquire at this level ever since. Thanks to a cultivated eye, he has bought in many instances from artists on the threshold of recognition.

Blanco, who has died since Carey came to know her, grew up in a potting and farming village, Santa María Atzompa, five miles from Oaxaca. From childhood on, she loved to play and work with clay. She made animals and ashtrays, and illustrated scenes from stories told her by her grandmother. While still young, she would carry her wares in a basket to the Oaxaca market. As she grew older she would occasionally take time during her weekly trip to the city to visit the archeological museum. Teodora had dropped out of grammar school, not liking it, and though she was intelligent she also was deeply superstitious. Devils and evil spirits were real to her, and she brought these to malicious life in her work. She also depicted animal spirits, *nahuals*, meant to protect her against the evil others. Side by side with her superstition there coexisted a true religiosity: Casey owns a Blanco nativity—manger, Mary, Joseph, Baby Jesus, wise men, animals, all delineated with loving detail. Creating other scenes and people typical of ordinary village life, she could express affection and kindness.

In a community where a majority of the inhabitants made pottery and clay figures, Blanco's were by far the most popular. She began signing them. Soon rivals were forging her signature. By the early 1970s, says Carey, the inexperienced buyer had to be very careful that work offered as Teodora Blanco's was actually hers. To the discerning buyer, however, there was rarely a question.

Two other artists in particular stand out in Carey's collection. Candelario Medrano, nearly 100 years old, no longer works, although members of his family still produce ceramic figures from molds he designed. As a little boy in Santa Cruz de las Huertas, a small village of toy makers in northwestern Mexico, Medrano was adopted by a toy maker and taught the art. Well into adult life he contented himself with turning out toys, such as whistles

The man mounting the horse on this table of assorted carved, painted figures is Emiliano Zapata, the revolutionary leader and popular hero. Everything here except the copper and mica lamp, made by Dirk van Erp in Oakland, California, circa 1910, is the handiwork of Manuel Jimenez.

in animal shapes, until a potter from another town suggested that he assemble a group of animals on an ark and then create something in a larger framework. After he had been making and selling Noah's arks for a year, Medrano had his first sight of the cathedral in Guadalajara. He was inspired to copy the cathedral in clay and fill it with worshippers. When this sold, he went on to houses, trains, buses, and groups of people talking, singing, and dancing. Meanwhile he continued making animals, some of them fantastic creatures with human faces. Among Carey's Medrano creations are a ship with passengers, a rooster, and a multi-story apartment house complete with tenants.

The third artist is a wood carver, Manuel Jiménez, now in his sixties. Carey has more of his work than anyone else's, most of it consisting of remarkably expressive animal figures, though there are human and angel figures as well. Jiménez has made a reputation not only as an artist but as a spiritual healer and counselor. When Teodora Blanco suspected that she was the target of malignant forces, whether directed against her by neighbors or devils, she would travel 30 miles to Jiménez' village for help.

One of Jiménez' major creations, owned by Carey, is a battle scene representing the revolutionary forces of Zapata versus the army generals. There are forty figures, some of them on horseback, plus cannon, houses, flags, and guns.

Through the sweep of Carey's collection, which includes a number of other artists, not all of them well known, the rich diversity of daily life asserts itself. There are weddings, funerals, births (a hospital scene shows a caesarean section in progress), marketplaces, and fiestas.

Carey feels his collection has now reached the point at which he need add nothing more. But . . . "I swear I'll never buy another piece." he says. "Then I run across something unique."

PERSONAL and PRIVATE

Covering the Walls

The late Adelaide Fuller, almost by accident, assembled possibly the premier private collection of American Impressionist and Realist paintings and drawings in the country. This was done simply by acquiring art to hang on the walls of her home, without thoughts of becoming a Collector with a capital "C." "She had the taste, the eye, the imagination," says her husband, William Marshall Fuller, a Fort Worth entrepreneur with interests in oil, ranching, banking, and investments. "I was fortunate in two things: first, I had the desire to support and help her, and, second, I had the wherewithal."

When the Fullers moved in the early 1950s into the house he still occupies, the walls were pretty bare. "We had very little in the way of paintings," Fuller recalls, "and my wife was motivated by the desire to have something to put up, and something she liked. She went to Antoinette Kraushaar's gallery in New York. Antoinette called her attention in particular to Maurice Prendergast." That was the moment at which the direction their collecting would take was determined. Mrs. Fuller had two Prendergast watercolors sent home with the intention of deciding with her husband which they would like to keep. It turned out that they couldn't part with either of them.

As Mrs. Fuller began to shop for more pictures, she became acquainted with the work of other American painters who, like Prendergast, were influenced by the French Impressionists. These and members of a group calling itself The Eight, known to its detractors as the Ashcan School because it depicted scenes of everyday urban life, were the artists the Fullers favored. Thus they found themselves collecting in a rather narrow but rich field, which, as time went on, was destined to become an important one.

Some of the artists acquired by the Fullers were Maurice Prendergast's brother Charles, Everett Shinn, John Sloan, Childe Hassam, Arthur B. Davies, William Glackens, Robert Henri, Ernest Lawson, George Luks, John H. Twachtman, and Theodore Robinson.

During the last years of Mrs. Fuller's life, the couple stopped purchasing. "It was discouraging," Fuller says today, "to look at something and say 'That costs $150,000,' when 25 years ago we paid $4,500 for a painting by the same artist from the same period. And besides, by then our walls were full!"

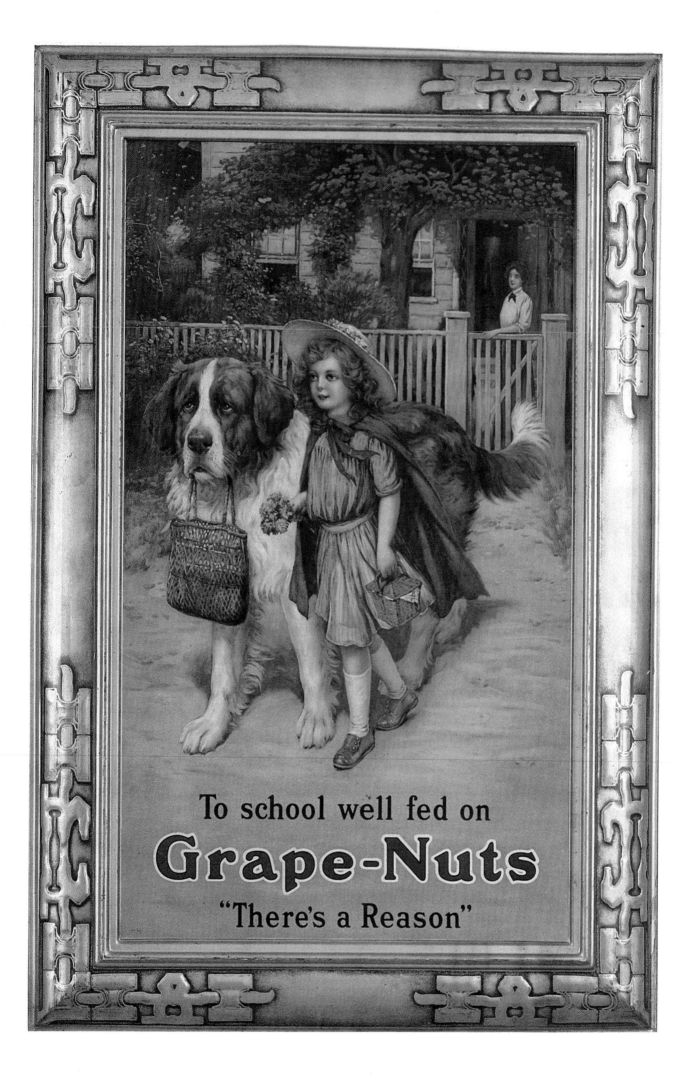

To school well fed on

Grape-Nuts

"There's a Reason"

PERSONAL and PRIVATE

Signs of the Past

Dallas collectors Kim and Mary Kokles can trace the path of history through their assemblage of advertising signs dating from about 1870 to the outbreak of World War I.

A good bit of America's past is preserved in advertising signs—some on paper, some on tin, some on wood. To an appreciative present-day eye it is evident that the artists who created the signs and the lithographers, printers, and others who had a hand in their reproduction were people of genuine talent.

As collectors of such signs dating from approximately 1870 to the outbreak of World War I, Kim and Mary Kokles of Dallas feel they have a front seat in history. This is not, to be sure, the textbook history of political leaders and great events but that of the daily life of ordinary citizens for whose patronage the nation's manufacturers were competing.

Mary was a collector of antiques until Kim introduced her to sign collecting. Originally, his interest had been old bottles. "A friend and I would go out to a dump in use around 1900 and dig them up," he recalls. "A big treasure hunt! Then I saw signs advertising what had been in the bottles, and it was a natural transition to start collecting the signs."

Big Boy was a popular soft drink around 1916. One of the Kokleses' signs urges: "Drink Ice Cold Big Boy—Highest Quality." Depicted is a kids' baseball game, the boys all in uniform and the member of one team leaning over a fence, holding a bottle of the stuff enticingly toward the viewer. Kokles cites this sign as representative of a particular type of advertising art in which the product is scaled out of all proportion to everything else in the scene. "If this bottle were as big as it looks," he says, "it would easily hold 60 ounces!"

"Have You a Little Fairy in Your Home?" asks a sign repeating a famous question of this century's early years. The illustration was equally famous: a little girl in a fur hat clutching a bunch of violets. The product was Fairy Soap, a big seller at five cents per white oval bar.

Comparing old ads with new, it is evident that certain appeals and ploys have remained constant. In the good old days as now, female beauty was used to sell beer and whisky. Fashionable women were pictured imbibing, pretty girls serving. The fair sex also heightened the allure of tobacco, sometimes by naughtily puffing away on a cigarlet, sometimes just by being part of the advertisement's mise-en-scène. Success in romance, often an implied bonus to anyone purchasing a specific product, is

suggested in one of the Kokleses' signs on paper: a lovely young miss and her swain are shown sharing a stick of Adams Tutti-Fruiti chewing gum. It has been stretched out into a long, spaghetti-like strand of which she has one end in her mouth, he the other in his. They appear to be in process of masticating their way toward a kiss.

Crude humor played a part in many signs. A well-dressed gentleman who has made the mistake of sitting down on a large carton marked Carter's Mucilage is trying to get off. A young boy has him by the hand and is making a Herculean effort to pull him loose, but this mucilage ("The Great Stickist," according to the slogan) is ahead of its time—every bit as unyielding as today's Krazy Glue.

Among collectors certain signs are prized as classics. In this category is the Kokleses' tin sign advertising Grape-Nuts. A girl—long brown hair, straw hat, green dress, red cape—is setting out for school accompanied by her faithful Saint Bernard. She has a bouquet in her right hand, what appears to be a lunch basket in her left. The dog carries her purse in its jaws. Mom stands at the gate before the house seeing them off. The caption beneath this idyllic tableau says, "To school well fed on Grape-Nuts." And below, in quotes: "'There's a reason.'"

Scenes of American life are always in demand, says Kokles, particularly pastoral scenes. Anything patriotic also has a built-in plus; Uncle Sam's appearance on a sign contributes to its value.

"Some people collect special types of signs," he notes; "brewery signs, for example. I personally don't care if the product is as uninteresting as shoelaces providing the graphics are good.

"The best lithography," he explains, "was done in the

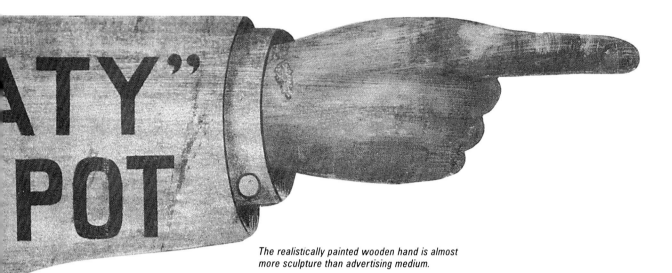

The realistically painted wooden hand is almost more sculpture than advertising medium.

1800s, up to the early 1900s. At the time we are dealing with, all the images were first rendered on stone. A sign on paper was produced directly from stone—a different stone for each color. If an advertisement had 26 colors, the paper would go from stone to stone to stone. The detail was unbelievable. To end up on tin, a sign had to be transferred to a rubber mat. The colors on tin jump out at you. It's essentially a lost art today; they can't reproduce it. The heart of my collection is tin, which is considered the most desirable, but I also have wood as well as paper."

Wood antedated tin in the service of advertising. Most wooden signs were for trades rather than products—an anvil, for example, proclaiming the presence of a blacksmith. Unusual among the Kokleses' wooden signs is a pointing hand emblazoned with the letters MKT. Quite a few of these had gone up in the town of Cleburne, in central Texas, at the time of the opening there of a new Missouri, Kansas & Texas Railroad depot; they doubtless helped thousands of passengers find their way to the "Katy" station. Though oversized and obviously flat, the hand has an almost real look, giving an eerie effect. It comes close to constituting a work of art.

The fact that the Kokleses are dealers as well as collectors has encouraged them to be broader in their interests than some fellow members of the Tin Can Collectors Association, or "Tin Can Club," who profess total indifference to wooden signs. (The T.T.C.A.'s original focus was exclusively on coffee and tobacco tins and the like, although this was expanded over the years to include anything lithographed on tin.)

"As for me," Kokles says, "the more I see of wooden signs, the better I like them."

PERSONAL and PRIVATE

Beaded Whimseys:
American Folk Art
or Kitsch?

In New York's Museum of the American Indian a small display of beaded whimseys carries an explanatory card saying, among other things: "The complete degeneration of an ancient art from the beautifully designed pouches into the strictly commercial articles made for sale at Niagara Falls around 1900 is all too evident in the exhibit."

Susan Mustard Roller of Austin, a historic preservationist, artist, and art psychotherapist, has been devoting a good part of her time in recent years to disputing such negative opinions.

But what are beaded whimseys?

No one knows the origin of the term. The objects themselves are articles featuring a unique three-dimensional beadwork, produced by Northeastern Woodlands Indian women as Victorian-era tourist souvenirs. Prior to European contact, these Indians employed dyed porcupine quills and moose hair for decoration. When glass beads became available, the beads were applied to the old quill-work designs and were substituted for the knotted moose hair in a traditional type of raised embroidery. Furthermore, as these European influences, especially needlework as taught in French-Canadian convents in the 1700s came into play, the Indians picked up the bold, new floral figures and combined them with other motifs from nature—even nature learned about second hand, such as elephants. Beaded whimseys, then, were a result of mixing these various elements.

Although some whimseys served as pin cushions, wall pockets, needle cases or picture frames, most had no utilitarian purpose. They might look like purses or be shaped like birds or pillows or canoes; essentially they were functionless additions—exotic and colorful—to the household clutter favored at that time. The fact that they were sold at Niagara Falls was a plus. Niagara being one of the period's prime magnets for travelers, the epitome of natural grandeur, what could be more romantically satisfying than a memento made by one of the Noble Savages living in the vicinity of the great cataract?

Susan Roller's introduction to whimseys dates from 1972 when she was a graduate student in art at Southern Methodist University in Dallas. Her friend and faculty advisor, Paul Rogers Harris, could show her a whimsey in a glass case but not answer questions about it. Within a week she had spotted another at a flea market and bought it

*Susan M. Roller of Austin regards her beaded whimsies,
Victorian-era souvenirs made by Northeastern Woodlands
Indian women and sold to tourists at Niagra Falls, as
intriguing examples of American folk art.*

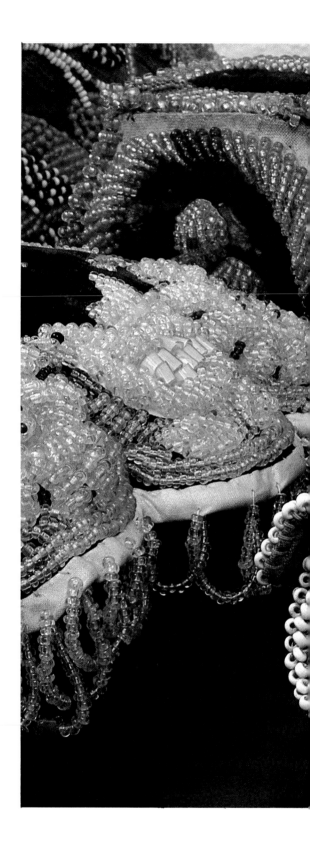

for ten dollars. "I thought it was serendipitous," she says, "finding a second work by the same long-dead artist in such a short time." Soon she came across a third, for which she paid five dollars; then a fourth for three dollars. On a trip to England she noticed them in shops and was told they were French—not a bad guess, considering their French influence. By now Roller realized that a whole group of artists had to be involved and eventually she found out who they were.

She also learned that those few students of the American Indian who were aware of whimseys disapproved of them because, as she says, "they don't look Indian, they were made by women, purchased mainly by women and sold as souvenirs." Moreover, as the card accompanying the Indian museum's display of whimseys would have it, they represent "the complete degeneration of an ancient art."

"I absolutely disagree," counters Roller. "I see them as the Indians' response to the collision of Indian culture with the white Victorian culture. In my art history training I learned that any time two strong cultures are mixed, a very vibrant art is often the result. These fit that description: when you are hit with a bunch of them, they are breathtaking. Indian and art and antiques scholars either don't know about them or are all gummed up with their own prejudices!"

Roller today owns about 400 whimseys dating from the late 1840s to the 1930s. She has found a few kindred spirits who collect them, including a woman in Scotland, but, thanks to her personal research, she figures she probably knows as much about them as anyone else. Even the handful of museums that own them have scant idea what they are and little apparent interest in extending their knowledge.

"It is time," Roller says confidently, "for beaded whimseys to occupy a place in American folk art on a level with quilts."

PERSONAL and PRIVATE

Remembering the Centennial

Among Bill Bain's Centennial treasures is a paper parasol sold to protect fairgoers from Dallas' searing summer heat.

1936 was an important year for the Lone Star State—its hundredth anniversary. Centerpiece of the programs and celebrations marking the milestone was a big Centennial fair in Dallas.

Bill Bain, a Houston general contractor and developer, not yet born when the fair began attracting thousands, may get as much pleasure out of that cheerful, gaudy show today as anyone did at the time. His colorful collection of Centennial memorabilia, accumulated over the past dozen years, almost certainly is the largest anywhere.

Bain observes just two rules in determining what belongs in his collection. The articles (1) must be in good condition and in their original state, without repairs, and (2) must bear some legend or logo identifying them as produced in connection with the Centennial. Objects meeting these requirements deck the walls and fill numerous shelves and drawers in the living room and dining room of his house. Visiting the Bains, one can easily get the impression of living simultaneously in the present and the past. The hundreds on hundreds of souvenirs, from a piece of sheet music, *Come on Down to Texas*, written and published by Samantha I. Tucker, to one of the fine felt hats presented to honored guests at the fair, make the Centennial seem very immediate.

Among other mementoes are a two-volume *Texas Encyclopedia* issued in 1936 by the Texas Historical Society, postcards (some of them written on and mailed) extolling the fair's wonders, salt and pepper shakers, ashtrays, cheap jewelry, Czechoslovakian plates illustrating Texas themes (the six flags, the Alamo, longhorn steer, the Spanish missions), a child's chaps and leather vest, a replica of a Colt .45 six-shooter, a miniature covered wagon, sets of decorated tumblers, a parasol sold at the fair (the summer of 1936 was baking hot), and dishes and bowls adorned with the state flower (bluebonnet). Other mementoes include walking sticks, a roll of tickets for a ten-cents-a-dance parlor known as "Joe's Night on the Yukon," a photograph of a table made by a shop teacher using woods from all the varieties of Texas trees (exhibited at the fair, not to be found afterward), a sunbonnet, license plate ornaments, and a brass doorstop. Thousands of different items were manufactured specially for the Centennial, most, though not all, sold or given away at the fair. Bain has lost count of how many of them have come into his possession.

Houstonian Bill Bain's Czechoslovakian-made commemorative plate is one of a series presenting Texas themes, such as the Alamo, Spanish missions, longhorn cattle, and native flora.

A wide range of interests have made Bain's house a veritable display case of Americana.

It was more or less by chance that he became a collector, and his concentration on the Centennial also is largely a matter of happenstance. "My dad was a pilot for Braniff for 30 years," he says. "I was a pilot for a couple, for Texas International. I would work three days and be off two. On free days, for something to do, I would go to flea markets." At the flea markets he started buying Centennial artifacts, because they were linked by a common theme and because they were inexpensive.

Bain also bought other things that caught his fancy. A glass-fronted cabinet contains some 80 or 90 pieces of "case" art, small cases made of gummed shellac and fibrous material forming a hard, brittle substance that was a forerunner of modern plastic. An artist-engraver would cut a design, often ornate, to be die-stamped on the plastic material. The result was a handsome dark carrying case for a picture. Some were rectangular or square, others round; the latter have come to be known as "oreos" after today's popular cookies. Manufactured between the years 1857 and 1865, the cases were in vogue during the Civil War. Men in uniform, the women they left behind, children and family groups appear in the stiffly posed daguerreotypes in this rare collection.

Wide-ranging interests including baseball, toy trains, fire trucks, and airplanes have made Bain's home a virtual museum of Americana, of which the Centennial souvenirs and the cases are the strongest components. Dominating one end of the Bain living room, and as American as a Norman Rockwell *Saturday Evening Post* cover, is a soda fountain complete with marble counter, glassware, and Coca-Cola tin trays sporting the likenesses of pretty girls. Bain brought the fountain sight unseen on the basis of a photograph sent by a friend in Denver, where an old-fashioned drug store was going out of business. Another friend who has a trucking company delivered it. It isn't hooked up to plumbing or stocked with ice cream, ice, or syrups; but even non-functioning, it adds the perfect final touch to this household organized around nostalgia.

Bain also collects case art, display objects made of gummed shellac and a fibrous material that was a forerunner of plastic.

A descendant of Wedgwood pottery founder Josiah,
Hensleigh Wedgwood of Dallas came by his interest in the
genre naturally.

PERSONAL and PRIVATE

Wedgwood's Wedgwoods

It would be difficult *not* to be at least a casual collector if your name were Wedgwood and you were employed by the great family enterprise that has given the world some of its finest ceramics.

Hensleigh Wedgwood, president of the company's American division in New York until his retirement and move to Dallas, owns an outstanding collection of Wedgwood. The truth is, however, that he originally did not set out to collect; he simply held onto certain articles that came his way while letting others go. The realization that, given his personal connection with what the Wedgwood factories had turned out over more than two hundred years, he should be building up a genuine collection came later. "I've kicked myself ever since that I didn't keep this piece or that piece which was particular or special," he says.

Actually, there seems very little ground for regret; once Wedgwood decided to become a true collector, he filled in enough gaps so that virtually all types of pottery and china manufactured by the firm since its founding are illustrated.

Josiah Wedgwood formed a partnership with the famous Staffordshire potter Thomas Whieldon in 1754 and began to experiment with bodies and glazes. Five years later, without Whieldon, he established the Wedgwood Pottery. The basis for his fame and fortune was laid with the development of an earthenware featuring simple, functional shapes and restrained floral or geometrical ornamentation—a fresh look for that time. Josiah's brother John, a bit of a diletante moving in London high society, introduced the Cream Ware to Queen Charlotte, who ordered a small service. When it arrived she was so delighted that she appointed Wedgwood Potter to the Queen. After its enthusiastic endorsement by Charlotte in 1765, Queen's Ware—the name it promptly acquired—went on to become one of Wedgwood's most popular and varied lines. In the sub-category of dairy ware alone were many special-purpose items such as butter churns, settling pans, storage jars, and skimmers. Hensleigh Wedgwood's collection boasts a representative selection of Queen's Ware, much of it distinguished by an appearance of airy lightness.

By 1769 Josiah Wedgwood was sufficiently prosperous to build a new factory in partnership with Thomas Bentley. Because ancient Greece was to provide the major inspiration for future output, and Greek vases were then thought of as Etruscan, the factory was called Etruria and its motto was "The Etruscan arts are reborn." Etruria as a trademark is found on a number of choice items in Wedgwood's collection, old and recent.

In the same year the Etruria plant was opened, the partners set up a workshop in London for enamel painting. Since workers skilled in the technique were scarce, it was necessary to train them. Much of the Queen's Ware was decorated with enamel, and it would continue to be employed in connection with other styles.

When Bentley died in 1780, Wedgwood took his sons and a nephew into partnership. Josiah was a forward-looking man, ahead of his time—in concern for the environment, for example, and in his support of the American Revolution and the abolition of slavery. Further, he had an artist's eye and solid entrepreneurial ability. While objects of beauty, utility, and charm—some of them innovative and setting new fashions—were produced throughout his lifetime and beyond, his *chef d'oeuvre* is generally held to be the Portland Vase, issued in probably 45 copies, of which only about 16 survive.

The original of this, disinterred outside Rome, is believed to have been made in Alexandria in the first century B.C. Acquired in 1785 by the Dowager Duchess of Portland, it was put up for auction after her death, with two determined bidders driving up the price. Finally, the duchess' son sent a note to his rival, Josiah Wedgwood, saying, in effect, "If you will stop bidding against me, I'll let you have the vase to copy," since it was known this was why he wanted it. The auction ended then and there.

An inveterate experimenter, Wedgwood spent four years figuring out how to reproduce the vase with its classical, white Grecian figures on a lustrous black background. Then the subscribers to the edition received their duplicates in the jasper ware that was a Wedgwood creation. These were pronounced "a correct and faithful imitation" by Sir Joshua Reynolds.

In its most familiar form, jasper comes in blue and white, although cups and saucers, medallions, sugar-and-cream sets, plaques, jewelry, vases, bowls, and other objects evoking a classical style also are found in yellow, green, or lilac. Hensleigh Wedgwood owns examples in all the colors. The medallions were a vehicle for portraiture, with prominent artists of the period modeling eminent personages whose likenesses would be valued by the public.

Black basalt was an earlier ornamental ware developed by Wedgwood, a refinement of a crude Staffordshire pottery known as Egyptian Black. This ware often served for portrait busts and had many other uses, as in vases, lamps, condiment sets, mugs, and plaques. The black basalt in Hensleigh Wedgwood's collection gives the impression of bearing out what his ancestor Josiah wrote of it: "The black is sterling and will last forever."

Other wares with which Wedgwood enjoyed success over the years included green glaze, marbled, cane, piecrust, and *rosso antico*, the last an unglazed red stoneware imitating that of Greek or Roman pottery. Only in its production of bone china did the company fail to maintain its usual lead in high fashion and its standard of excellence. Around 1805 a competitor, Spode, started marketing this fine, translucent porcelain made of clay mixed with bone ash. Josiah Wedgwood had died in 1795 and Josiah II, "nominally in charge of the factory," in Hensleigh's description, "was not the least bit interested. He had a lot of money and was retired, a country gentleman, in Dorset. He went up to Staffordshire (where the factory was) about twice a year, in a red coach drawn by six white horses—like royalty. He was cautious, silent, forbidding. The salesmen in the London office kept saying, 'Hey, get on the ball! We've got to have bone china! Everybody else is doing it.' He wouldn't, so Spode and others captured the market.

"Finally, in 1812, he gave the order to produce bone china. It required new equipment and new techniques. Then the quality wasn't frightfully good. It was not nearly as translucent as it should have been. He gave it up in 1821." In the meantime Wedgwood also made stone china, less fine than bone, but discontinued its manufacture after an even shorter period.

From a collector's point of view the result of these two abandoned efforts is challenging, since Wedgwood bone and stone china are now relatively rare; but Hensleigh Wedgwood does have examples of both.

Rarities of other sorts figure in the collection. It contains pieces from a one-of-a-kind dinner service made for the Duke of Bedford, displaying the ducal crest. (The present Duke of Bedford has a good portion of the rest.) There are also pieces from a service owned by Charles Darwin's grandfather Erasmus Darwin, a doctor and good friend of the first Josiah Wedgwood. A game pie dish commemorates a moment in history, the year 1806, when Britain suffered a flour shortage. The cover of the baking dish was designed to simulate the crust that was missing from the pie.

Though it is increasingly difficult to find anything rare, Wedgwood and wife Barbara frequent local antique shows, and at least once have been rewarded by discovering a pattern he had never seen before.

As to why a scion of the Wedgwoods should have chosen to retire to a part of the world so distant from England, the answer proves quite simple. "When I was president of the American Company," Hensleigh Wedgwood says, "we had a good customer in Dallas: Neiman-Marcus. Their buyer became my wife."

PRIVATE goes PUBLIC

All for Love

Briton John Piper designed the costumes for an early 1950s production of the opera Don Giovanni.

Collecting is only part of Robert L. B. Tobin's fervent involvement with theater, ballet, opera, graphic art, and books. He once underwrote a San Antonio production of *Don Giovanni*, which he himself designed and directed. Also in his home town, he played the starring role of the egotistical, acidulous Sheridan Whiteside in *The Man Who Came to Dinner*. He was seen but not heard in a New York Civic Opera presentation of Hans Werner Henze's *The Young Lord*, miming a mute. And with his mother, the *doyenne* of San Antonio society, he met the costs of a new staging of Stravinsky's opera *The Rake's Progress* at the Royal Opera in Covent Garden, London. That Stravinsky became a personal friend was a serendipitous spinoff.

Quite possibly, collecting is a substitute in Tobin's life for participating more fully in the creative process. If so, no lingering regret over unfulfilled dreams is discernible to the casual eye. The white-maned, bearded six-footer appears to have a dedicated scholar's knowledge of everything he has acquired and to thoroughly relish the pleasures of connoisseurship.

"I love passionately every single object," he says. "Every object has meant something to me. It has meant in many cases having a spirited time at an auction." As a frequenter of London auctions, he often stayed at the Westbury Hotel in Mayfair. His regular bartender there had just enough idea of what he was up to to say one evening, "I'm afraid this is very impertinent, Mr. Tobin. You're not English furniture and you're not French silver. What are you?"

What Tobin became as a collector was pretty much determined when he was a student at the University of Texas in Austin and needed a set of books for a paper on stage design. Though the library had them, the books were not available to him, so with the easy assurance of the affluent, young Robert bought his own. He continued to buy books, some because they dealt with the performing arts or with aspects of visual art such as perspective (of major importance in theatrical history), others simply for their excellence as examples of bookmaking. In addition, he purchased maquettes of stage sets, along with designs for sets, costumes, and various related materials.

"Affluent" is perhaps an inadequate adjective in relation to Robert Tobin. His family, high on the Texas social scale, became one of the state's wealthiest after his father, Edgar, a flying ace in World War I, started photographing

A watercolor and pencil work depicts a street scene set in "West Side Story" designed by Oliver Smith, its monumentality bearing down on the tragic young lovers in Leonard Bernstein's musical.

geological anomalies from the air. This mapping service requested by the Humble Oil Company provided such valuable information that the elder Tobin figured it could be sold through the oil industry and also be adapted for certain other businesses. Accordingly, he gave up his profession, teaching, to establish what has since become three companies: Tobin Aerial Surveys, Tobin Surveys, Inc., and Tobin Research. When Edgar Tobin died in a plane crash in 1954 with that other aviation pioneer Tom Braniff, he left his wife, Margaret, and nineteen-year-old Robert an enormous fortune. Robert has continued to run the Tobin enterprises; by maintaining close telephone contact with his staff in San Antonio, wherever he may be, he has freed himself to pursue his other interests.

These take him frequently to such places as Santa Fe, New York, Spoleto, and various European capitals. Besides being on the board of the McNay Museum in San Antonio, he is on those of the Metropolitan and Santa Fe operas and serves as vice chairman of the drawings committee of Manhattan's Museum of Modern Art.

His connection with the McNay is particularly close, not only because it is on home ground but also because

it boasts a Tobin Wing, opened in 1984, the year of his fiftieth birthday. This elegant addition to an already beautiful Mediterranean-style building, the onetime residence of art patron Marion Koogler McNay, was made possible by a $1.4-million gift from his mother. Incorporating two floors linked by a great curving staircase, the wing was intended to accommodate the entire Tobin collection. This includes some 8000 illustrated and/or rare books, many of them first editions, and more than 20,000 paintings, drawings, posters, and stage models. It is hard to pick standouts from such a vast assortment, but mention must be made of an original set of engravings by Palladio, the sixteenth-century architect whose villas in Italy set the style for many English country houses; the manuscript libretto of *Parsifal* signed by Wagner; Picasso's designs for the Ballets Russes production of *Parade*; an original set of Diderot's *Encyclopedia*; and proof sheets from Blake's illustrated *Book of Job*. Books on the early history of flight pay homage to Tobin's father.

Actually, a number of choice items from the collection have not made their way to the wing, remaining in one of Tobin's several houses: the big one in San Antonio, an

adobe in the historical section of Santa Fe and a Park Avenue brownstone in New York.

Standing in his Manhattan house, Tobin gestured at the books, pictures, and other objects and said, "I'm constantly transferring things from New York to the McNay." But, to judge by the visible evidence, he must also be just as steadily replenishing the stock in New York.

An eye catcher in the dark-paneled living room was what appeared to be a mockup of a divided staircase about two feet high, with lower and upper landings, constructed of wood and metal and centered on a long table. As design it was interesting, but its function, if any, was obscure. Tobin explained that it represented "an exercise of some sort" required of French architectural students in the nineteenth century as a prerequisite to obtaining a baccalaureate degree. While it presumably had nothing to do with the theater, it made one think of certain stage sets or of Shakespeare's Globe.

There were books, sculptures, and paintings in the house that would have been worth close inspection, but Tobin was more inclined to talk about the wing in San Antonio and what is accessible there to the public. A series of exhibitions has been mounted "to give people an idea," as he says, "of what the collection is about." First came a show titled "Eugene Berman and the Theatre of Melancholia." Berman, a Russian-born artist and scene designer, was one of the youthful Tobin's first idols and, later, his friend. Berman spent many years in Rome and there produced some of his most characteristic work, marked by a brooding preoccupation with a largely imaginary past in which mouldering ruins were an important element. He married the Hollywood actress Ona Munson, whom he often employed as a model in dramatic poses based on characters from mythology or Shakespeare. Some of his finest stage sets were for the Metropolitan Opera.

The second San Antonio exhibition, "From Word to Image," had only limited success, according to Tobin. Each show in the series has been accompanied by a catalogue with a foreword by Tobin, and for this one he wrote, " 'From Word to Image' connotes a firm commitment to the concept of the validity of a visual response to the stimulus of a text, whether this be a theatrical production, a cinematographic exercise or a typographic answer to the challenge of the dramatic text. A text thus inspires creative expression." In other words, the exhibition was meant to illustrate how artists working in one medium or another may base their creations on something written. For reasons Tobin could not fathom, this concept eluded the public. "No one caught on," he says, "though I thought it was

clear enough." Even those confused by the theme, however (or by the way Tobin stated it), would have found interesting things to look at. Many of them were plates from seventeenth-century books depicting stage sets for operas or elaborate spectacles. As the catalogue notes, such entertainments grew out of significant celebratory occasions of royalty and the nobility, which were commemorated by elaborate books called *livres des fêtes*, a number of which are in the Tobin collection. Seeds of subsequent theatrical design, costuming, choreography, and architecture as well, are to be found in these sumptuous volumes, often enlisting the talents of major artists. The exhibit also included theater-related paintings, drawings, and prints and, in a category of its own, a necklace made by sculptor Louise Nevelson to be worn by special guests attending an opening night in St. Louis of Gluck's *Orfeo and Euridice*, for which she had created not only the decor but also the design for the libretto.

Other exhibitions have dealt with scene design in the American theater, centering on the influence of Robert Edmond Jones; with perspective, especially as "discovered" in Renaissance Italy, and applied there and elsewhere to theater and art; with Leon Bakst and Alexandre Benois, principal designers for Serge Diaghilev, and with Benois' son, Nicola, and niece, Nadia Benois, inheritors of the family tradition; also with opera and works on paper.

In introducing the show of works on paper, Tobin wrote that its title, "Paperworks," was "deceptively explicit" in that it "both reveals and conceals, rather like a smart bathing frock on the Riviera.

"The common denominator," his foreword continued, "is, obviously, paper. The uncommon aspect is what is done to, done about, done with paper.

"Obviously, the book is our tribal common ground."

Among books displayed in whole or through individual pages in "Paperworks" were a Gutenberg Bible, the Bruce Rogers Bible ("a conscious effort to produce *the* edition of the King James version"), a Kelmscott Press Chaucer, and various volumes showcasing the works of such modern artists as Sonia Delaunay, Aristide Maillol, Joseph Albers, and Jim Dine. In addition, there were etchings, collages, drawings, watercolors, and other graphics unrelated to books or to theater. The point of this exhibit, like that of "From Word to Image," may have been lost on some viewers. Tobin reported with some puzzlement that a woman had come up to him after taking it in, and said, "Isn't it interesting? All the works are on paper."

Sheaves of Wheat *by Vincent Van Gogh, oil on canvas, 197/8″ by 393/4″, 1890.*

PRIVATE goes PUBLIC

The Wendy Reves Show

"We didn't start out collecting. We were trying to make the villa beautiful. And when I would see something, I'd say, 'Oh, you know, darling, this would be beautiful for such and such a room.' That's why I asked them to make an adaptation, because every single thing . . ."

Wendy Reves trails off, gesturing all-inclusively at her surroundings. The "adaptation" is a re-creation of the interior of Villa La Pausa on France's Côte d'Azur, home for many years of the Reveses, Emery and Wendy. It was this villa that the couple beautified with paintings, graphics, and sculpture by the likes of Daumier, Rodin, Van Gogh, and Degas, Middle Eastern carpets, rare china, glass, and silver, fine furniture, and distinctive decorative objects. Now the surviving partner of the marriage is showing a visitor through the Wendy and Emery Reves Collection, exhibited in a scaled-down version of the house that was its original setting. This transplanted Villa La Pausa occupies the major part of a new decorative arts wing at the Dallas Museum of Art.

The actual villa had been built for Coco Chanel by the Duke of Westminster in 1927; it was bought by the Reveses 26 years later in a state of disrepair. Chanel was an ambiguous figure during World War II, continuing a relationship, begun earlier, with Westminster's successor, a German baron. Some of her actions suggested that she was a collaborator with the Nazi occupiers, others that she was using her connection with the baron to aid the Resistance. In any case, once the war was over, the doyenne of *haute couture* and *parfumerie* followed her lover to Switzerland and abandoned La Pausa.

Not only did the Reveses restore the badly rundown property, they turned it into a showplace and a favored home away from home of world leaders and celebrities. Guests included Churchill, Noel Coward, Somerset Maugham, Greta Garbo, the Rothschilds, Rose Kennedy, Konrad Adenauer, the Duke of Windsor, and Graham Sutherland. Emery Reves himself had achieved celebrity with the publication in 1945 of his *The Anatomy of Peace*, which became an 800,000-copy bestseller. No less an advocate than Albert Einstein endorsed this book, which urged the creation of a world government as the only way to avoid the global devastation of nuclear war.

Reves, a Hungarian Jew (born Revesz), had become a British subject in 1940 with King George VI, Churchill, Lord Beaverbrook, Clement Atlee, Anthony Eden and Lord Samuels as his sponsors. The good will of such distinguished personages had been earned through his accomplishments as a political journalist and pioneering entrepreneur in the form of a newspaper syndication of his own creation. As a freelance reporter, the young Reves had often sold the same interview with some statesman or important official to papers in different cities, an innovative practice at the time. It occurred to him that the same thing could be done with articles by the prominent figures themselves. They might, in fact, be distributed internationally, communicating the views of a country's leaders to readers in others. Reves's main interest, then as subsequently, was in trying to promote peace through improved communication and cooperation among nations. Accordingly, at the age of 26, Reves founded the Cooperation Press Service in Paris. He chose Paris rather than Berlin, his prior base of operations, because his departure from that city had been a flight for life: a phone call from his cleaning woman had warned him that the secret police were after him. Both as a critic of the rising national Socialist party and a Jew, Reves would be in jeopardy if he remained in Germany.

Later he was to learn that his Berlin apartment had been broken into and ransacked. Already a sophisticated collector, he lost a number of paintings by German abstract expressionists.

Three years after establishing his syndicate, Reves represented some 120 clients, mostly European officials, and had agreements with approximately 400 newspapers in more than 70 countries.

Winston Churchill, in the period leading up to World War II, was living through his "wilderness years," a low point in his previously distinguished career when he had no public position or power. To afford him a platform, Reves offered him a contract with Cooperation Press Service but had to give him better terms than anyone else to obtain his signature. From 1936 on, thanks to Reves, Churchill managed to make his opinions known to his compatriots and the world at large. Ironically, the syndicate's very success eventually began to cost it a substantial part of its audience. Churchill's anti-Nazi rhetoric and Reves's own sympathies created uneasiness in countries threatened by Hitler, now Germany's head of state, and increasing numbers of papers stopped using the service. Nevertheless, when Churchill attacked Neville Chamberlain's appeasement of Hitler at Munich, deriding his fellow Briton's claim that sacrificing Czechoslovakia to the Third Reich would ensure "peace in our time," Reves still was able to get worldwide coverage for the scathing riposte.

Toward the end of the 1930s Reves commissioned and published several books, all exposés of Hitler and his regime. After war broke out, Churchill advised him to move to London, but Reves remained at his post in Paris until the Germans crossed the French border. With storm troopers on the city's outskirts and refugees clogging the escape routes, he again fled for his life, driving a luxurious new Hispano-Suiza he had just managed to acquire for the little money he had on him—a car destined for another pur-

chaser who obviously was not going to be able to claim it. Ending up on a British destroyer anchored in Bordeaux harbor, Reves prevailed on the captain to contact the War Office in London. Churchill, recently elected prime minister, lost no time in directing the captain to see that his friend was transferred to a British cargo ship, which soon deposited him in England.

It was then that Reves became a British citizen. For a short time he worked in the Ministry of Information. Though seriously wounded when a bomb struck his flat, he set to thinking how he might best serve his new government—and the free world in general. It seemed to him that American participation in the war was essential, and that with his background and skills he could help bring it about. With Churchill's blessing, he made his way slowly and arduously to New York, via Lisbon, arriving aboard ship in February 1941.

From then until 1945 he devoted himself to articles and letters to the editor seeking to influence American opinion and, once this country was in the war, to elucidating the issues involved; also to writing two books, *A Democratic Manifesto*, stating the case for Britain in the present conflict, and *The Anatomy of Peace*. He was 41 years old, successful, and about to meet the woman he would want to make part of his hitherto work-oriented life.

Wendy Russell's background could hardly have been less like Reves's. Born in the small East Texas town of Marshall to David and Blanche Russell, a charming, improvident barber shop owner and his attractive, much put-upon wife, she was six years old when her parents divorced. Blanche had an aunt and uncle who had given her a home when she was orphaned. After the divorce they again took her in, along with her daughter. Gifted with musical talent, Blanche taught at a local college and, increasingly, accepted out-of-town engagements as pianist, organist, and vocalist. The uncle seems not to have been too pleased to find himself with another child to look after, but the aunt was loving and encouraged Wendy to be self-reliant and ambitious.

In 1930 when Wendy was in her teens, her mother moved her to another small town in Louisiana, where an oil boom of sorts was in progress. The only work Blanche could find, as a kindergarten teacher, barely put food on the table. By leasing a furnished house and taking in boarders, she improved their circumstances considerably and provided a warm, family-like environment in which Wendy blossomed.

This happy interlude ended when Dave Russell reappeared, now a used-car salesman in San Antonio, and persuaded his ex-wife to remarry him and move again with Wendy to his new home base. The second attempt at mar-

Custody of the Child *by Winston Churchill, oil on canvas, 24¾" by 29¾".*

riage worked no better than the first, although this time the couple remained together.

While still in high school, Wendy was offered a part-time modeling job by a local merchant, but within months she received what seemed an even better offer—to marry a recent West Point graduate enrolled in flying school at nearby Randolph Field. Acceding to her mother's request to wait a year before deciding, she saw her young lieutenant reassigned to Hawaii, then on her seventeenth birthday sailed off to join him.

The birth of a son a year later did not make Wendy's marriage any more successful than her mother's, and within another few years it was over and she was back in San Antonio resuming her modeling career. To take advantage of the greater opportunities in New York, Wendy left her son in her parents' care while she headed east. (She and the son today are estranged.)

Breaking into the big time did not prove easy, but when she realized that bright makeup and platinum hair were no longer the approved look, she toned down her image and won her chance, eventually becoming one of the most popular models in the country.

In 1940 Wendy met and married Paul Baron, staff conductor for the Columbia Broadcasting Company. This

union proved unequal to the strain of a busy social schedule and conflicting job demands. By the time Wendy made the acquaintance of Emery Reves she was again free for a new, finally fulfilling, relationship, even though she was slow to recognize the opportunity when it presented itself. Their first encounter came about by chance when Reves stopped to talk to a businessman friend with whom Wendy was having cocktails. The war had ended and *The Anatomy of Peace* had made Reves a well-known figure. As for Wendy, her face was familiar to him through magazine covers and ads. Two days later while Wendy was walking down Fifth Avenue with Blanche, Reves happened along again. It occurred to Wendy that he and her mother might hit it off, and when he phoned the next morning to invite Wendy to dinner, she suggested that he come by her place for drinks and then take Blanche out. The suggestion was politely rejected.

Two years were to pass before Russell and Reves were to see each other again, years in which Wendy built up a fashion-related business and starred in a nightclub turn while Emery pursued his publishing activities and promoted a new organization for world federation. They finally were brought together as dinner partners by a mutual friend. Wendy was surprised to observe that the seemingly shy Reves dominated the conversation with informed opinions on a wide range of subjects from politics to economics to art and theater. When he escorted her home and asked if he might see her again, she had no hesitation in saying yes.

Before long the two were frequent companions. On her first trip to Europe, on business, Wendy was met by Emery at the dock in Southampton with a car and chauffeur. Before leaving England Emery bought a Jaguar convertible for touring the French countryside in style. As time went on, new scenes, new friends from Emery's sophisticated circle, and exposure to concerts and museums combined to broaden Wendy's horizons. And her mentor had someone with whom to share the amenities he had earned.

After five years spent in hotels, together or separately, where business or pleasure took them, Wendy wanted to settle down. Emery, though predisposed by past experience to favor a relatively rootless existence, yielded to her need for a stable home. They were ready to be seduced by La Pausa.

It was after they had rehabilitated it, filled it with their own possessions, and lived and entertained in it for more than a decade that the couple, looking to the future of the house, decided to marry. Emery was suffering from a chronic heart condition that ultimately would kill him, and as his widow and heir Wendy would have full legal standing to carry out their joint wishes regarding La Pausa's contents. What they had in mind was to give these to a museum that would exhibit them in surroundings approximating as nearly as possible those for which they had been chosen by the Reveses. In honoring that requirement the Dallas Museum of Art retained Edward Larrabee Barnes as architect to design a wing that contains half a dozen adaptations (to employ Wendy's word) of La Pausa rooms in an integrated unit evocative of the villa overlooking Monte Carlo and the Mediterranean.

This Texas Villa La Pausa was unveiled to the public in November 1985. Costs of construction ($6 million) and of transferring the contents of the house in Roquebrune-Cap Martin to Dallas had been met by a group of benefactors. The collection, numbering 1,429 items, was valued at $35 million, doubling the worth of the museum's previous holdings. Outstanding among the Reves contributions were approximately 70 paintings, other works on paper, and

sculptures, with a heavy concentration on French Impressionists and Post-Impressionists. The roster of artists included Cézanne, van Gogh, Gauguin, Daumier, Rodin, Corot, Toulouse-Lautrec, Renoir, Sisley, Monet, Manet, Vlaminck, Redon, Bonnard, Courbet, Seurat, and Vuillard. Other gifts—Chinese porcelains, rugs from Spain and the Middle East, furniture dating from the Middle Ages onward, antique silver, Venetian glass, and old wrought iron—extended the museum's range for the first time into the area of decorative arts. A kind of shrine to Winston Churchill was set up in a small room, displaying mementoes of his visits to La Pausa.

Early reaction to the Reves Collection in its special setting was not wholly favorable. Jim Schutze, for example, writing in the *Dallas Times Herald*, grumbled, "It's absolutely immorally egotistical. . . . Mrs. Reves, bless her heart, generous though she has been to our deserving city, is a former model and widow of a wealthy man. She is not an architect. She is not an artist. She is not a statesman, a tycoon, a soldier or a saint in the formal religious sense of the word (as far as we know, the Holy Mother did not appear to Mrs. Reves at La Pausa and order her to have a replica of her house built in Dallas, Texas, let alone cure her of anything).

"To reproduce her home as an entire wing of a museum of art is to exalt her as if she were all of these things, of which she is none. She is this: *a possessor of stuff*. . . ."

Shutze was compelled to acknowledge, however, that "there is some staggering art in that collection. And it is really interesting to see it in the non-institutional setting of a home. Standing in a hallway looking at a painting right next to me over a small cabinet, I had to pinch myself and think, 'That's that *Sheaves* painting by van Gogh!'"

Wendy Reves was on hand to direct the placement of every object before the wing's opening. Now she is back again from France, supervising a crew making alterations in the earlier arrangements. "We had to work so fast last time," she explains, "we couldn't get it all right. Yesterday I made a great many changes."

Passing through a large unfurnished space, not part of the villa proper but leading to it, Mrs. Reves gestures toward wall-hung rugs from the Middle East and Spain, richly patterned. In La Pausa these were on the floor, and "people had to take off their shoes and put on slippers to walk on them. The head of the textile museum in Washington came to see them," Mrs. Reves continues. "He spent the weekend on his hands and knees. He said it was the greatest collection in private hands. Fabulous."

The re-created entry hall is a small foyer with a welcoming air. Whenever Churchill visited, Mrs. Reves would clear the long table on the right and lay out the assorted headgear he had accumulated during previous stays. He had a weakness for hats and caps and each morning would choose one for the day. Beneath the table is a wrought-iron door knocker, eighteenth-century French. "I've always loved iron, ever since I was a little child," says Mrs. Reves, "I don't know why." On the wall hangs a lyrical Redon pastel, *Flowers in a Black Vase*; a table under it holds a stained plaster cast of an 1860 sculpture by Jean-Baptiste Carpeaux, *Ugolino and His Sons*. The artist, not widely known today, was a precursor of Rodin, less coolly classical than some of his contemporaries.

The Wing's "great hall" is modeled on the formal space in which large parties for heads of state and other dignitaries were held. On view are the van Gogh *Sheaves of Wheat*, a peaceful picture painted the same month the artist committed suicide; Vlaminck's vivid landscape *Bougival*; two Rodin marbles; dozens of wrought-iron door hinges; and Graham Sutherland's gold and silver *Cross of Ely*. The somewhat rough-hewn expressionistic cross is a moot object: the cathedral that commissioned it rejected it and writer Bill Marvel, then art critic at the *Times Herald*, referred to it as "one of the ugliest crosses in all Christendom." Standing 43½ inches high, it consists of a square central plaque, with four hand-like protrusions ("the hands of God"), on a vertical support atop a pedestal; toward the center of the plaque is a small crucifix set against a heart. The highly polished precious metals of the surfaces reflect light and make the sculpture hard to ignore whether one likes it or not.

The great hall is two stories high (though "the one at the villa is much bigger"), and Mrs. Reves leads the way up a flight of stairs to a gallery lined, rather eerily, with dozens of Reves's empty frames. "We treated frames like objects of art," says Mrs. Reves. Her husband, it seems, had developed a strong bond with an elderly man in London named Wiggins, a dealer in frames, and there were days when Reves would leave their hotel at six in the morning to visit him (Wiggins lived some distance out) and not return until late at night, "tired and dirty." If he had found three frames, he would be content. "It took something like 18 years to make this collection," says Mrs. Reves.

Alongside the staircase are more examples of Mrs. Reves' wrought iron—latches, hasps, fireplace implements, and the like. Old iron is very difficult to clean, explains our guide, and what is on view is the fruit of 14 years of labor. "We had a maître d'hotel and his assistant," Mrs. Reves says, "and a chef and *his* assistant—four boys. From the time that everything was cleaned up after the guests had had their lunch until let's say five-thirty when they had their dinner, they had free time. It was too short a time for them to go home and do something, so they would sit in a cave and clean the iron. It was all rusty—thick rust like that, every single piece. I would say to them, 'If you do one piece a month, I'm happy.' And every time they would finish a piece we would lacquer it, and they would bring it on a cushion—they were so proud—and I would give them a kiss and we would have a bottle of champagne."

Descending a staircase at the opposite end of the gallery and crossing into an antechamber leading to the dining room, Mrs. Reves says, "As you go through you will see there are Renoirs and everything very far away, and people complain. And so we have been bringing a few selected things closer—we call it art of the month. First we brought out the two Renoirs from the salon which everybody was angry because they couldn't get up and smell 'em." Now on view close up is table silver, rare Queen Anne, a collection painstakingly assembled over the years, eight pieces here, a dozen there.

There is more Queen Anne silver in the dining room, some in a vitrine, the rest on a large table laid for a dinner party: 18 place settings all from the same maker, the same year, the same family. A Mrs. Howe in London, the silver merchant from whom the Queen Anne service was purchased, is certain there is no other complete set extant. The china, glassware, lace place mats, and accessories on the table also are of exceptional quality. The glassware, Mrs. Reves says, is all eighteenth century, very rare and "impossible to assemble." Before the impossibility became manifest, the Reveses managed to find 13 of everything.

The dining room walls hold several notable paintings including a Vuillard and Seurat's *Grassy Riverbank* of 1882, the latter foreshadowing his masterpiece *Sunday Afternoon on the Island of the Grande Jatte.*

In Mrs. Reves' bedroom, *la Belle Chambre*, are vitrines with more than 50 pieces of Chinese and Chinese export porcelains dating from 1686 to 1800. On a large pedestal stands a striking Five Vase Garniture of the K'ang Hsi period (1662–1722), each vase decorated with multicolored motifs from nature on a black background.

The bedroom, Victorian in feeling, is furnished entirely in elaborate nineteenth-century French and English papier-mâché, black lacquer overlaid with floral designs. The chair seats are fabric-covered except for two, done startlingly in tiger skin. Heavy burgundy draperies are matched by a canopy over the head of the bed. Two glass cases contain a collection of 34 fans; there are 46 more still in the villa. A large Degas pastel of female bathers on the banks of a pond or stream, the central figure combing out the hair that cascades down over her face, is the dominant work of art.

Mrs. Reves' eye perceives that one of the rugs in *la Belle Chambre* is crooked. This would not have been permitted at La Pausa; she steps over the velvet rope in the doorway to join four members of the museum staff and Flavio, a gentle middle-aged retainer from the villa. Together they roll up the rug, turn it around, unroll it again and tug this way and that until it lies straight. Now that she is in the room, she cannot resist looking critically at the way small objects are disposed on tables, moving and regrouping them so that they will be more easily visible beyond the velvet barrier.

Four or five visitors to the wing arrive as Mrs. Reves is about to step back into the public area. "Hello, how are you?" she greets them. "I'm Wendy Reves. I'm glad to see you. Come in—enjoy it! We're working. I'm here trying to make it even prettier." The visitors appear slightly taken aback. This is more than they expected for their three-dollar admission fee. "Have you been here before?" Mrs. Reves asks.

"Not in your part," says one of the women.

"Have you been to the other side yet?"

"No."

"O-o-h, then please, go to the other side and then I'm

going to get out of here, so that you can have it in the serenity that I meant it to be. Okay? Go and look at the other side, then we'll all get out of your way. I hope you like it!"

More visitors follow immediately. Mrs. Reves, still on the far side of the rope, again introduces herself. A man in the group wants to know if people really slept in a bed like that. "I did," she says, adding, "It's not the same mattress, it's a fake. But this is my room, exactly the way it is—except that I had that painting [now on an easel] on the wall, and the paneling is smaller than it is in the villa. Everything is smaller here." She explains that things need rearranging because of the haste with which they were installed. In fact, she confides, the museum director thinks they got off to such a good start because she was still working the evening of the opening, and everybody came and said afterward, "My God, Wendy Reves was there and she was working, moving the furniture around!" More or less satisfied with the bedchamber, Mrs. Reves steps out over the rope again. The tour resumes, much as before. During the course of it one sees the eminently unimportant, such as Winston Churchill's cane, his monogrammed crystal brandy snifter and several of the landscapes and seascapes it pleased him to paint at La Pausa. A gallery devoted to drawings, however, shows off some of the great names of nineteenth- and early-twentieth-century French art—Daumier, Toulouse-Lautrec, Renoir, van Gogh, et al.—at their most felicitous. And the large and handsome salon and inviting paneled library offer rewards both for their contents—furniture, paintings, books, lacquered and inlaid boxes, and other art objects—and the manner in which these contents are integrated into harmonious living spaces.

The furniture is European, ranging from fifteenth-century Gothic to seventeenth-century collectors' cabinets incorporating such components as tortoise shell, gilt metal, and wood-and-ivory marquetry, up to painted Victorian.

Among the canvases are five Renoirs, two of them portraits of one of his favorite models, Lise; a Monet rendering of the Pont Neuf; two Manet still lifes; another by Courbet in

Wendy Reves' re-created bedroom at the Dallas Museum of Art is Victorian in feeling with its florid black lacquer furnishings of papier-mache from nineteenth-century England and France.

Still Life with Apples on a Sideboard *by Paul Cezanne, watercolor, 19⅛″ by 24⅞″, 1902–06.*

which apples, a pear, and pomegranates stand out with an almost palpable reality; a Graham Sutherland portrait of Emery Reves; a Corot portrait; landscapes by Gauguin, Sisley, and Cézanne; a Cézanne still life, and a Pissarro portrait and street scene.

A Gauguin portrait vase of a woman friend constitutes an unusual example of his work in ceramics, limited to the period prior to his departure for Tahiti. And not to be overlooked are various rare textiles.

Toward the end of the guided tour Mrs. Reves suggests a coffee break in a storeroom. There on a wall hangs an oil portrait of her by Graham Sutherland. It's not on display, she says, because "everyone at the museum hates it." Why?

"If you'll look at it carefully, you'll see it's out of proportion."

There's a story that goes with the picture, and Mrs. Reves tells it. Sutherland was a great friend of the Reveses and accepted a commission from Mrs. Reves to paint the portrait of Emery displayed in the library. Emery in turn wanted him to paint Wendy. "And in those days," she ex-plains, "I was young and very pretty. Graham said, 'She's too pretty; I can't. I just don't paint things that are pretty. I just can't do it.' Emery said, 'Thank you very much! That means I'm not pretty.' And so we waited and we waited, and every year Emery would reapproach him and he would always say, 'Well, I can't do it, I just can't.' And so finally we were in Switzerland and Emery found a postcard with the most wrinkled, horrible old peasant woman from the mountains. He wrote on the back, 'Dear Graham, This is the way Wendy looks today.' And of course Graham succumbed and decided to paint me. Then what happened was, he was very very ill, and knew it, and he rushed everything. If you look at it, from here up it's me. And from here down it is his wife, who came to my shoulder. In other words, the lower part of the body doesn't go with the upper part; it's foreshortened. And the people here in the museum all hate it because they all think I'm very attractive. . . .

"Graham was crazy about it, he really was. And I said to him when I saw it the first time, 'Graham, it's so big!' And he said, 'What can I do? You're bigger than life.'"

PRIVATE goes PUBLIC

Saving Old New Braunfels

New Braunfels, approximately 25 miles northeast of San Antonio, was founded by Prince Carl of Solms-Braunfels. He was "33, handsome, and a first cousin to Queen Victoria," writes T. R. Fehrenbach in his history, *Lone Star*, (Macmillan, 1968), adding: "He was also something of a monumental fool, though he undoubtedly meant well." The prince's fatuousness was illustrated by the way he presented himself to the planters who had preceded him to the area, "displaying both aristocratic snobbery . . . and intolerance toward the system of Negro slavery. This, his appearance in full uniform with sword and decorations, and his retinue of servants, valet, architect, cook, secretary, and someone hired as a 'professional hunter,' strained even the famous Texas hospitality."

Solms-Braunfels had been sent to Texas in 1844 by a group of Prussian nobles incorporated as the Society for the Protection of German Immigrants in Texas. The organization was dedicated to creating a new German fatherland in America, which would constitute an overseas market for products manufactured in the old fatherland. At the same time it was hoped that, under the society's benevolent eye, the emigrants might be helped to lead richer, freer lives than had been possible for the average farmer and industrial worker back home. Inducements such as free transportation, free land, and a free log house were offered to people who might not otherwise think of pulling up roots in Germany to try their luck on the far frontier, and thousands of peasants and laborers responded. The high-minded project fell disastrously short of its objectives. To begin with, it was undercapitalized. Then, the imigrants ran into brutal weather, much of the land allotted to them was unsuited to farming, and, even worse, the men who had sold it to the society for distribution didn't own it.

Little wonder that Prince Carl resigned his commission and returned to his princedom. What was remarkable was that a sizable remnant of the settlers did manage, over the course of time, to make a reasonably good life for themselves in an area that had become a German graveyard.

When W. H. and Nan Dillen moved from Kansas City to San Antonio in 1935 to escape the harsh Missouri winters, they knew little about New Braunfels or its origins. Exploring the country around them, however, they soon discovered the community and were charmed by its houses

Left & Below: One of the Dillens' prized garage-sale finds is a walnut and pine wardrobe believed to have been made by Franz Stautzenberger. The date 1860 is inscribed on the cartouche.

Bottom: W. H. and Nan Dillen restored the Breustedt house, circa 1858, in New Braunfels and furnished it with exquisite examples of early Texas furniture. In 1982, the Dillens deeded the house and its furnishings to the city, which opened the house as the Museum of Texas Hand-Made Furniture.

built in ancient *Fachwerk* (half-timber) style. Being in the decorating business, they also became interested in the furniture still to be found in some of the residences and sometimes in stores, for sale as used rather than as antique pieces.

In 1946 the Dillens moved again, to New Braunfels. Feeling that the special quality of the little town (population then around 7,500) should be preserved, they bought several properties. One was a former bakery, which became their new shop. Another was the rundown Comal Hotel, vintage 1900, named after the county of which New Braunfels is the seat. "It was two stories, eight rooms to a floor," Bill Dillen recalls. "The first floor had 13-foot ceilings, the second floor 11-foot. An unfinished basement, with a dirt floor, ran the whole length of the building. We bought it from the descendants of the original owner, modernized it and renamed it the Prince Solm. We kept the furnishings mostly Victorian."

His voice takes on a note of regret. "We sold the hotel in 1977, and the furniture with it, with the understanding it would remain in the building. But the purchaser defaulted and the finance company in Austin auctioned it all off. It went all over the country."

In another salvage operation, the couple purchased a house that was about to be demolished. Dating from around 1858, the Breustedt house stood on 14 acres. The Dillens deeded three acres, including the structure's site, to the New Braunfels Conservation Society and had the house itself moved to what was by then a preferable spot on the remaining acreage. They proceeded to restore it as a home for themselves, furnishing it with local pieces.

In the course of seeking these out, and incidentally fostering an appreciation of them by others, the Dillens became authorities on Texas handmade furniture. "When Nan and I first moved here," Dillon recalls, "we didn't know about the fine cabinetmakers." Then they began to see examples of their work. Eager for background information, they studied census and other records. In a list of approximately 7,000 German immigrants between 1845 and 1847, 46 gave their occupation as cabinetmaker. After some had turned to farming or continued on their travels, some half dozen remained to practice their skills in the area. These have become known individually, almost as friends, to the pair who have carefully studied their output.

Generally the furniture is made of either yellow pine or walnut, the later in plentiful supply locally. The pine had to come from Bastrop, 60 miles away. The style of the furniture, in common with that at Henkel Square and Winedale, (see p. 168) shows the expected German, often Biedermeier, influence.

Canvasing estate and garage sales as well as scouring the shops, the Dillens have aimed for representation of all the top cabinetmakers. The quest has provided moments of excitement, as when Dillen spotted an antique German-style stool at a garage sale and asked its owner if she had anything else of the same type. The woman took him across the street to the unoccupied house of her mother, recently deceased. There he recognized a wardrobe as being a mate to one by Franz Stautzenberger and illustrated in the book, *Texas Furniture: Cabinet Makers and Their Work*, 1840-1880, by Lonn Taylor and David B. Warren. (Publication of the book by the University of Texas Press in 1975 had been sponsored by Ima Hogg, who died two years before it appeared.) Each wardrobe had a cartouche inscribed with a date. The one bought by the Dillens had been made in 1860, a year before that in the photograph. A little detective work disclosed that after Stautzenberger had built the original wardrobe for some neighbors, his niece, about to marry, had asked for one just like it.

While they were assembling their furniture collection, the Dillens were also collecting early pewter, mainly German, and white ironstone, made in England between 1843 and 1860 for export. While some of the pewter and ironstone had found its way to pioneer New Braunfels, the Dillens had had to go far afield—visiting antique shops coast to coast—for most of what ended up in their home.

In 1982 they deeded the house, the greater part of its contents, adjoining buildings, and the land to the Braunfels Foundation Trust. The Heritage Society was formed to manage the property, and in 1985 the Museum of Texas Hand-Made Furniture was opened to the public.

The Dillens, who had moved to an apartment in town, took with them a large covered vegetable dish that had belonged to Bill's great-grandmother, the basis of their ironstone collection. Today, both in their seventies, they are honored citizens of a town that has grown to almost 25,000 —a town still in close touch with its past, thanks in great measure to their efforts.

Fully furnished rooms at the Breustedt House, complete with textiles and decorative art, provide an accurate representation of the region's top 19th-century cabinetmakers.

Guadalupe Banner, *cut tissue paper, Puebla, State of Puebla. 16" in height.* In collecting Mexican folk art, the late Robert K. Winn of San Antonio focused on religious art, particularly that pertaining to the celebration of Christmas. Banners such as the one shown, generally in pastel colors or white, are strung across streets and doorways at Christmastime. The white-rose motif of the Guadalupe Banner harks back to the story of Juan Diego, from whose cape white roses cascaded when he recounted his vision of the Virgin to the head of the Church in Mexico.

PRIVATE goes PUBLIC

Olé!

Robert K. Winn's lifelong collection of Mexican folk art, now in the hands of the San Antonio Museum Association, includes examples from acclaimed Oaxacan ceramist Teodora Blanco, such as the depiction in clay of the Holy Family. This contemporary artist has developed a distinctive style in which decorative details are "embroidered" on a figure's basic form.

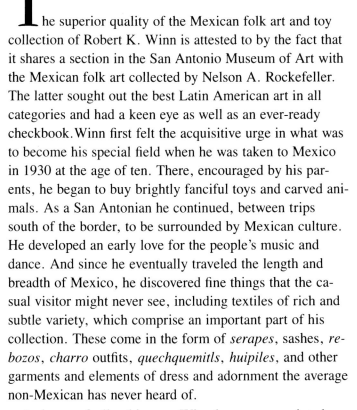

The superior quality of the Mexican folk art and toy collection of Robert K. Winn is attested to by the fact that it shares a section in the San Antonio Museum of Art with the Mexican folk art collected by Nelson A. Rockefeller. The latter sought out the best Latin American art in all categories and had a keen eye as well as an ever-ready checkbook. Winn first felt the acquisitive urge in what was to become his special field when he was taken to Mexico in 1930 at the age of ten. There, encouraged by his parents, he began to buy brightly fanciful toys and carved animals. As a San Antonian he continued, between trips south of the border, to be surrounded by Mexican culture. He developed an early love for the people's music and dance. And since he eventually traveled the length and breadth of Mexico, he discovered fine things that the casual visitor might never see, including textiles of rich and subtle variety, which comprise an important part of his collection. These come in the form of *serapes*, sashes, *rebozos*, *charro* outfits, *quechquemitls*, *huipiles*, and other garments and elements of dress and adornment the average non-Mexican has never heard of.

As he was feeling his way, Winn became acquainted with collectors in Mexico, particularly Humberto Garza of Monterrey, and with interior designers and others who drew upon folk art in their work. Influential among these

was fellow San Antonian Alexander Girard, whose collection is housed at the Museum of International Folk Art in Santa Fe, New Mexico.

Winn himself grew to be an accomplished artist, and he taught art history at Trinity University in his home city. Toward the end of his life he owned and ran a gallery specializing in Mexican art. His own work evinced a sophisticated design sense and also reflected his folk-art orientation. From time to time he was called upon to organize and curate exhibitions of Latin American art in local museums and elsewhere. One such show, drawn from his personal collection, traveled to various museums throughout the Southwest. Titled "Viva Jesus, María y José," it depicted what Winn described as "the Mexican salutation to Christmas—a time of joy, of celebration, and of national fiestas." As the collector pointed out, the Christmas folk art of Mexico started with a pragmatic purpose: to teach the Christmas story to the Indians in simple and appealing fashion.

In 1979, around the time of Winn's death, his collection was exhibited in Explorers Hall of the National Geographic Society in Washington. Afterward it passed to the San Antonio Museum Association.

Incidentally, the San Antonio Museum has a third collection of Mexican folk art in addition to those of Winn and Rockefeller. This was contributed by Joe Nicholson, a San Antonian, and is complementary to the other two, consisting largely of musical instruments and contemporary toys and miniatures. In all, the museum now owns approximately 8,000 pieces of Mexican folk art, making it a magnet to aficionados of the genre.

PRIVATE goes PUBLIC

The Remarkable Mr. De

Everette Lee DeGolyer, who died in 1956, left many legacies.

As the world's leading petroleum geologist, he succeeded in locating important oil deposits that fueled industrial and technological growth and made Americans the most mobile people in history. (The Potrero Llano #4 in Veracruz, Mexico, the most productive oil well ever, was drilled in 1910 on a site chosen by the 24-year-old DeGolyer.)

An innovator and mathematical whiz, he pioneered the science of geophysics, helping to refine the techniques by which hidden sources of oil were identified.

A corporate leader, he headed or participated in the formation of companies (the Amerada Corporation, Texas Instruments, and Texas Eastern Transmission) that played a major part in setting the course of the energy business well past his own lifetime.

In World War II, working for the government, he applied his expertise to the vital task of conserving oil, making an invaluable contribution to victory and the survival of the free world. Later, he continued to build for the future as an adviser to the Atomic Energy Commission.

Finally, as a student of history and lover of literature, DeGolyer assembled three notable book collections, all of which he made available to the public.

The first signs of the collector's instinct were perceptible in the months preceding the Potrero #4 discovery. Young Everette, taking advantage of what a strange country had to offer, began to accumulate Mexican fossil specimens and to seek out books dealing with Spain's conquests in the New World. Both the fossils and the books were sent by him to his teachers at the University of Oklahoma. It was at the university, opened in 1892 in Norman thanks to Oklahoma's new-found oil wealth, that Kansas-born DeGolyer had studied geology. In order to go to work for the Mexican Eagle Oil Company he interrupted his schooling, but he retained close ties with his campus mentors, knowing he would be back soon to complete his requirements for a degree. His alma mater was always to command his affectionate loyalty and would eventually become the recipient of his library on the early history of science.

Everette was in love with a Norman girl, and in 1911, after both had won their diplomas, he took Nell Virginia Goodrich back to Mexico as his bride. There she stayed until coming down with malaria while carrying their second child (their first, a son, had been stillborn). Everette sent Nell home to Norman where she could be properly cared for and deliver the baby, a healthy daughter. Four months after Virginia's birth Everette became one of many Americans to leave the revolution-torn Mexico of 1913 on orders from the United States government. The British firm that owned Mexican Eagle valued Everette too highly to let him go, and assigned him to make a study of oil prospects in Cuba, after which he was summoned to London with his family for talks with the head of the company. Next he was dispatched on a mission to Spain, but before he got past Paris, World War I broke out and not only was he prevented from continuing his journey but he barely escaped internment as a German. Finally convinced that he was American, the authorities permitted him to return to London. (In later years DeGolyer was to make several visits to Spain in a fruitless search for oil, on occasion running into his art-collector oilman friend from Dallas, Algur Meadows.)

It was in London that the impulse to begin collecting books took firm hold. Browsing in Hatchard's in Piccadilly, he came across a first edition of *The Pickwick Papers* and bought it for three pounds. This turned out to be a choice first edition in that it contained an error: the frontispiece illustration showed a signboard over the inn with the proprietor's name spelled Tony Veller instead of Weller. DeGolyer considered himself hooked as a collector from that point on.

With Europe now impractical as a theater for his operations, he worked out an agreement with his employers to look after certain of their interests in the States, in Mexico (where Americans seemed less threatened than a year ago), in Cuba, and the Caribbean.

The DeGolyers were able to return to Norman, and for a while led a relatively uneventful life. But soon Everette was again spending more and more time out of the country. He had begun to think of setting himself up as an independent consultant, and when the company asked him to open a New York office, he persuaded them to accept an arrangement whereby he would consult with the firm six months of the year and be free the rest of the year for other work. The DeGolyers did, however, move to the New York area. Once there, Everette was subject to the special en-

ticements that a big city holds for the collector.

Lon Tinkle in his biography of DeGolyer, *Mr. De*, tells how as a boy in Oklahoma working in a china shop, Everette had wondered if he would ever be able to afford beautiful objects like those around him. Now, having taken a cut in income while dipping deep into reserves to buy a fine house in New Jersey during a wartime housing shortage, he was drawn to Tiffany's and its temptations. On one of his repeated visits, a work of sculpture caught his eye, a two-foot-high bronze by Solon Borglum, brother of Gutzon—later to become famous for Mount Rushmore. The sculpture portrayed a bearded, weary prospector, seated on the ground in the shade cast by his horse, holding his hat in one hand and mopping his brow with the other. Like the boy he used to be, Everette once again felt poor in relation to something he saw as beautiful and out of reach. In 1916, $600 was a lot for someone with no money to spare.

His encounter with *The Prospector* took place on a Saturday. When he got home he was so full of his experience that he couldn't stop talking about it. According to Tinkle, Nell told him, "You go back Monday and get it."

On Monday morning he had an appointment with a man who wanted some oil property evaluated. When asked how much he would charge, DeGolyer had his answer ready: "Six hundred dollars."

The Prospector was the first of many art objects DeGolyer was to acquire, though over the long run books remained his primary concern as a collector.

New York was of course a rich source on which he drew at first for books about all aspects of Mexico and about the American Southwest, with emphasis on Indians and their clashes with whites. As time went on he bought—often in first editions—such authors as Conrad, Dickens, Hardy, Lamb, and Melville. Annual trips to London afforded further opportunities to add to his library. Many of the books found or ordered there also had to do with Mexico and the Southwest, also with political and military figures important in Mexican history, among them Santa Anna, Maximilian, and Juarez.

Early in 1924 DeGolyer purchased an outstanding, and costly, Mexican library collected over many years by one William Baker Stevens. In the summer of the same year he indulged his taste for belles lettres by spending $500 each for first editions of Stevenson's *New Arabian Nights* and *A Child's Garden of Verses*. Writing a check for the Mexican collection, he remarked, half jocularly, that he would no doubt have to move his family to a bigger house to accommodate it. There were now four children, three daughters and Everett (without the final "e") Lee, Jr. DeGolyer did in fact build himself a Tudor mansion in Montclair, New Jersey, shortly thereafter. One of its features was a rock garden in which many of the rocks, along with fossil specimens, were souvenirs of his collecting over the quarter century since he had made his first shipments from Mexico to the University of Oklahoma.

Well known by now, in triple capacity—as collector, authority on Mexico, and able writer of technical literature on oil and geology—he was invited in 1928 to contribute the entry on Santa Anna to the *Encyclopedia Britannica*. In a subsequent *Fortune* article on salt dome exploration for oil deposits, a seismographic method developed under his leadership, he evinced great skill at making abstruse matters intelligible to the lay public. But he continued to favor acquiring and reading what others had written over making his own mark as a writer.

The relationships DeGolyer formed with rare-book dealers tended to be long lasting. In 1928, the year of his *Britannica* piece, he bought his first book from a New York specialist in Western Americana, Edward Eberstadt. This is the same man, a German immigrant, whose business, passed on to his sons, was taken over in 1975 by John H. Jenkins III of Austin. The correspondence between purchaser and seller through the years shows the ripening of a genuine friendship. It paid reciprocal benefits: Eberstadt gave DeGolyer first crack at choice items falling into his hands, and DeGolyer tipped Eberstadt off on investments. Also, during the Great Depression the millionaire seemed to be making a special point of keeping the orders flowing, and once, in 1937, he answered a call for help by wiring $750 to Eberstadt on account against future purchases.

Later that year Eberstadt wrote him a letter in which he asked, "Do you remember way back in '29 when the old stock market went fluey and ruin and disaster stared us all in the face? I expect you do, but perhaps you don't remember that in that fatal time, and with the ship apparently sinking, you ascended the bridge, kicked the captain overboard, and for some perfectly insane reason gave thought to one poor guy way down 'tween decks a-hiding under a bunk, a-trembling with fright, and praying to God for the storm to pass over. The gent who had so suddenly got religion was me. I refer to your hefty order which came on that calamitous day. I need not tell you that I shall never forget it."

James F. Drake, also in New York, and H. W. Caldwell of Dallas were other dealers who became valued suppliers of DeGolyer's needs. They learned that he knew exactly what he wanted and how much it was worth. After his death Caldwell recalled meeting him for the first time and thinking him the best-dressed man he had ever seen.

In the 1940s DeGolyer's focus as a book collector began to shift to the field of science and the history of science. He still added to his store of first editions and works on Mexico and the Southwest; and another collection that had been accruing for decades continued to grow, one consisting of Mexican paintings, pre-Columbian artifacts, and Indian blankets. These occupied a special "Indian room" in New Jersey and, later, a similar room in the Dallas house the DeGolyers built in 1936 and where Everette was to spend his last 20 years.

During this period of maturity and stability both the DeGolyers entered into the cultural life of the community, one or the other of them assuming commitments with the Dallas Symphony, Margo Jones Theater, Arboretum Society, Planned Parenthood, and the public library. In 1941 DeGolyer bought, and for 15 years owned, *The Saturday Review*. With his respect for books and the free exchange of ideas, it is not surprising that when efforts were made to remove certain titles from the local library shelves, he insisted that the board and staff stand firm. Similar attempts to force conformity on *The Saturday Review* were met with equal resolve. Besides undertaking new business ventures, DeGolyer accepted the offer of a distinguished professorship at the University of Texas, where he helped restructure the geology department. His call to government service in World War II put an end to that stint of teaching (he was to lecture later at Princeton and elsewhere), but he showed his ongoing interest by a series of gifts to the university. He transferred title to the bulk of his literary first editions, including one of *Alice in Wonderland*, and to rare volumes of Whitman, Kipling, Melville, Shaw, and Dickens. He also presented the campus library with more than 1,200 other books and manuscripts, many of them especially interesting for idiosyncratic reasons. Such, for example, was a copy of a novel inscribed by its author to a friend and mailed to him the day before publication. The novel was *Man of Devon*, the author John Galsworthy, the friend Joseph Conrad. A great deal of technical material went to the Petroleum Reference Library of the geology department.

In correspondence with the university librarian, DeGolyer stipulated that his books and manuscripts should not be maintained intact as a unit, which he felt would limit their usefulness. He wrote, "Any method of handling the books which makes them most useful and most available to the library is satisfactory to me."

Part of DeGolyer's motivation in assembling his library on the history of science was to be able to present it to the University of Oklahoma, where it would serve as backup to a new course in this subject. He had long felt a general lack in science education: students concentrated on particular areas of science—biology, medicine, physics—but were not given a grounding in the growth of the scientific method nor helped to see the individual parts in relation to the whole. Of course just finding the books was not enough for DeGolyer. When possible, they must be rare or first editions. By 1955, the year before DeGolyer's death, the library contained some 10,000 items. If there were any doubt of its being preeminent in its field, the question had been set to rest a couple of years earlier when the librarian of the great MIT science collection, making a comparative study, discovered that the University of Oklahoma had 40 percent more books and endeavored to buy some of its duplicate copies.

DeGolyer's alma mater, however, did not reap all the benefits he had intended. Because he planned to write a history of the oil industry, he kept for reference purposes still another of his collections, reputedly the world's finest geology library, which eventually was supposed to become part of the university's science library. He died without making legal provision for the gift; thus the books on geology, along with his great collection of history and literature pertaining to the Southwest, remain the property of the DeGolyer Foundation in Dallas. The geology library is to be found in the Science Information Center at Southern Methodist University. SMU also is the repository for the bulk of the Southwest collection, and the university's law library accommodates close to 1,000 law-related volumes donated by DeGolyer. The DeGolyer home and surrounding acreage on White Rock Lake, sold to the city of Dallas by SMU, to which it had been bequeathed, are part of the city's newly developed arboretum.

The impulse—or compulsion—to collect was passed to the next generation by DeGolyer, Sr. though apparently in somewhat less insistent form. DeGolyer, Jr., who died in the seventies, focused on the history of transportation, chronicled primarily through books and photographs. SMU provides housing for his collection along with the treasures that have come to it from the remarkable man who was his father.

The Worcester porcelain collection amassed by Mr. and Mrs. Harris Masterson III and given to the Houston Museum of Fine Arts ranks as one of the finest in the world. The Duke of Gloucester deep plate, circa 1770, is made from the soft-paste porcelain developed by the English and French to compete with German manufacturers.

A World of Worcester

A sauce tureen, cover and ladle from the Worcester Porcelain Manufactory in England dates between 1775 and 1780, the age of all Worcester pieces in the Masterson collection.

There are certain things about Worcester porcelain you learn to recognize, according to Harris Masterson III of Houston.

"First, if you hold it up to the light, it flouresces green. Then, the way the glaze was applied on the bottom is distinctive. And you can tell the work of different decorators by their palettes and brush strokes. One of them, named Giles, executed some of the richer enamel paintings in the 1760s."

A distinct advantage to Worcester as a collectible, in Masterson's view, is that it does possess such recognizable attributes. "You feel safer buying it than other porcelains that have been faked a lot," he says.

Masterson, a sixth-generation Texan now more or less retired from activities involving oil, cattle, and land, bought his first piece of Worcester in 1943. "I always liked porcelain," he says, "and I was attracted to Worcester." His wife, Carroll, sharing his interest, encouraged him to become serious about it. He admits he didn't need any urging. "There's so much variety, you could go on collecting forever and ever and never complete it."

By the same token, it is next to impossible to adequately describe Worcester. Decorations range from landscapes to flowers, fruits, exotic birds, oriental scenes (adapted from the ware's original Chinese prototypes), animals, fish, and French courtiers or simple rustics at play. The color range has every hue and tint, from muted to bright.

It's not easy when looking at Worcester to remember it as a commodity that figured in a hard-fought commercial war. Made of white clay and soapstone blended to translucency, smooth to the touch and gracefully ornamented, it suggests delectable meals at tranquil eighteenth-century tables. Yet, precisely because good porcelain had such agreeable associations and happened to be difficult for occidentals to produce, the competition among European manufacturers was intense.

How the Chinese made it was a mystery to the Europeans who imported it. In 1709, after much experimentation, a formula for a comparable hard-paste porcelain was developed in Meissen, near Dresden, Germany. Unable to duplicate or approximate this, French and English ceramists came up with a soft-paste variation, generally a mixture of white clay, ground glass, and sometimes powdered bone (from which came the name bone china). Substituting soapstone for the glass, the Worcester Porcelain Company began turning out high-quality china in 1751 and to this day holds a commanding position in its field. The earlier pieces tend to be the simplest, both in form and embellishment, no doubt because those who made them were still learning the techniques. These are commonly held to be the most desirable. The factory opened in 1751, and Masterson's collection is entirely from that year to 1775.

In 1971 the Mastersons presented part of their by-then sizable collection to the Houston Museum of Fine Arts. Subsequently they made further gifts, buying desirable new examples of Worcester as they came on the market and passing them along to the museum so that its holdings would be as complete as possible.

To date the Mastersons have turned over more than 700 pieces, ensuring that the museum's collection of Worcester porcelain rank as one of the finest in the world.

PRIVATE goes PUBLIC

Robert and Elizabeth in Waco

The collection of Elizabeth and Robert Browning memorabilia assembled by Dr. A.J. Armstrong, longtime educator at Baylor University in Waco, is displayed in a library-cum-museum on the Baylor campus.

That the world's largest Browning collection should be located in Texas, midway between Austin and Dallas, is already something of an anomaly. To chance to visit it during a tornado alert adds to one's sense that the assorted memorabilia of Robert and Elizabeth Barrett Browning, gathered mostly from Italy and England, have ended up in somewhat exotic territory.

Devotees and students of the two poets, however, will be amply rewarded if they make the trip to Waco where the Armstrong Browning Library stands on the campus of Baylor University. And any feeling of inappropriateness or incongruity is likely to vanish as they walk up the stairs of a stately bronze-portaled temple as solid as the Victorian virtues, a safe haven against any tornado that might strike, and a dignified repository for the mementoes of the pair who, in their day, charmed and thrilled an international public.

In 1881, 20 years after Elizabeth's death, and eight years before Robert's, the first Browning Society was formed in London. Others blossomed elsewhere, many in the United States. The Armstrong Library was independent of these, originating in a private collection. The collector was Dr. A. J. Armstrong, who for 40 years (1912–1952) was chairman of the English Department at Baylor and who, shortly after joining its faculty, presented his prized holdings to the university. Subsequently he and fellow Browning buffs made further substantial contributions.

At the beginning, the collection was maintained in a special Browning Room in the university's Carroll Library. On trips abroad while he and his wife shepherded students on culture tours, Armstrong sought out paintings, furniture, letters, and other relevant objects and materials. Well before 1951 when the present library, built at a cost of more than $1.5 million, was dedicated, the collection had outgrown its original quarters. Today it stands as a model of a library-cum-museum in which architecture and decoration combine to provide an ideal setting for the appreciation of particular creative talents and their work. A special salon was created for furniture, books, portraits, china figures, and other items associated primarily with Elizabeth. A vitrine holds one of the few handwritten copies of her *Sonnets from the Portuguese*, love poems to Robert. (This was a dual-purpose title: it made the book sound like a work of translation, thus tending to protect the

privacy of the author's feelings, while at the same time it employed Robert's pet name for her. Because of her dark complexion he called her his "little Portuguese.") Numerous details throughout the building are tied, in special ways, to the Brownings' writings. The panels of the bronze entrance doors depict subjects from ten of Robert's poems. Fifty-four stained-glass windows, said to be the largest number in a secular building anywhere, also relate to poems by one or the other. A popular favorite is a Pied Piper of Hamlin window (after Robert's verses) found in the Research Hall. Robert's first great success was with poems, dramas, and miscellany published under the title *Bells and Pomegranates* (meant to indicate the "alternation of poetry and thought"), and there are bell-and-pomegranate decorative motifs in the grand, marbled entrance lobby with its lofty painted ceiling, and in profusion elsewhere. In front of the building is a statue of Pippa, the poor Italian child heroine of Robert's *Pippa Passes*, whose happy song changes the lives of those who hear her as she passes by:

> *The year's at the spring*
> *And day's at the morn;*
> *Morning's at seven;*
> *The hillside's dew-pearled;*
> *The lark's on the wing;*
> *The snail's on the thorn:*
> *God's in his heaven—*
> *All's right with the world.*

Besides the literary materials available in the second-floor Research Hall and third-floor Research Complex, many are displayed for the casual visitor strolling from room to room. Tender communications between the celebrated couple, first editions of their books, theater programs for plays by Robert—mostly unsuccessful—and letters to and from noted contemporaries are on view. So, too, are well-stocked music cabinets, articles of attire or adornment (a cross and a topaz brooch, for example, given by Robert to Elizabeth), the desks at which they wrote, a series of photographs of Robert at different stages and paintings from the walls of Casa Guidi, the Brownings' longtime home in Florence. All these and more evoke the interwined lives that figured in one of the best-loved personal stories of the nineteenth century. Symbolizing that story is a pair of clasped hands, their hands, cast in bronze by the American sculptor Harriet Hosmer. The hands are the dramatic focus in a cloister, part of the Foyer of Meditation.

Elizabeth, the eldest of 13 children, grew up a semi-invalid under the domination of a tyrannical father. So jealously possessive was Edward Barrett Moulton (he took Barrett as last name after the death of his maternal grandfather) that he forbade any of his eight sons or five daughters to marry, on pain of being disowned. When Robert, whose poetry Elizabeth admired, wrote to express his enthusiasm for poems she had published, a friendship began that was to ripen into love. Fearful of angering her father, Elizabeth only gradually allowed herself to acknowledge the depth of her affection; but at last she yielded to Robert's persistence and married him in a secret ceremony. Soon afterward the couple fled to Florence. Her health improved markedly and she gave Robert a child, Robert Wiedemann Browning, who was to develop into a talented painter and sculptor. (Examples of his work are in the library; his father was a frequent subject.) The marriage lasted 15 idyllic years, then Elizabeth, who was six years older than her husband, died. Robert returned to England, to live out most of the rest of his life an honored figure. His masterpiece, *The Ring and the Book*, was published during this period. Filling four volumes, the longest poem in the English language, it re-creates a horrendous murder in seventeenth-century Italy from twelve points of view, making it a kind of Western *Rashomon*. Although Robert would spend several autumns in Venice, he never again set foot in Florence. When he was buried in Westminster Abbey there was strong public sentiment for having Elizabeth disinterred for burial alongside him. Their son, however, decided her grave should not be disturbed.

Not everything that Armstrong owned of the Brownings found its way into the library during his lifetime. He took delight in wearing a signet ring of Robert's, a ring now behind glass.

He had other satisfactions, too, not vouchsafed the average person. Inscribed photographs are testimony to the friendship he enjoyed with the late Katharine Cornell and Brian Aherne, who as Elizabeth and Robert in Rudolph Besier's *The Barretts of Wimple Street*, scored a tremendous hit on Broadway and in cities across the country.

PERSONAL and PUBLIC

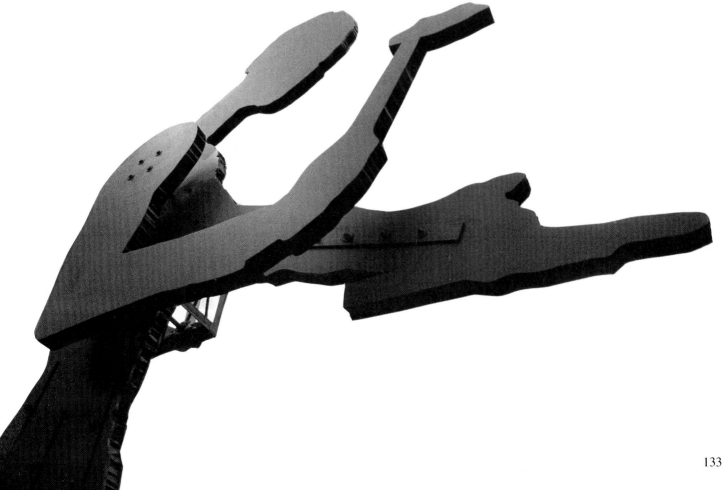

PERSONAL and PUBLIC

Barbed Wire Men

Drive up to the tidy house of Frank and Violet Smith in Keller, a community north of Fort Worth, and you will know without checking the street number that you have arrived at your destination, the home of a serious barbed wire collector. Out on the lawn a few feet apart stand two matching markers, stone posts topped by balls approximately three feet in diameter made of barbed wire wound tightly.

Smith is a retired locomotive engineer whose son Mark attending a junior college in Kerrville, Texas, in 1979, inspired him to turn collector. Each student in the engineering department, Mark included, was asked to add at least one new specimen to its barbed wire collection, and when the young man came home on a visit he and his father went searching. They found a roll of single-strand wire known as Sunderland Kink. Smith Senior kept a piece for himself, and from then on was committed to the quest, ever on the lookout for other varieties.

About halfway between Fort Worth and Austin some ten years earlier, another leading barbed wire collector was born. Gene Prickette, today tax collector and assessor for McLennan County, was at that time an appraiser for the former tax collector. The two men traveled over old rural roads, and Prickette sized up houses and established their value for tax purposes. In some of the remoter spots, land was fenced in with kinds of barbed wire rarely seen in modern times. The tax collector had been collecting examples of these and would occasionally add a new one.

"That started my interest," Prickette says. "I began doing it, too."

Barbed wire collectors abound in the Lone Star state. They have their own organization, the Texas Barbed Wire Collectors Association, and their own literature including the monthly *Barbed Wire Collector* and a *"Bobbed Wire' Bible*, updated every few years, cataloguing all known forms of the prickly product.

Smith undoubtedly speaks for the great majority of his fellows when he says that what makes barbed wire fascinating is history. "You've got to get into history," he says. "Just to collect barbed wire . . . that wouldn't last long."

It may come as a surprise to the uninitiated, but Texas lagged behind neighboring states in accepting barbed wire. This was because Texas longhorn cattle were so tough that

Frank Smith of Keller displays his barbed wire
collection—each strand labeled, dated and priced—on
specially designed wheels.

The earliest example of barbed wire comes from
Persia and is easily identifiable because it is made
from twisted camel's hair and thorns.

few people could conceive of their being deterred from going wherever they wanted by a barrier of wire—even wire with sharp prongs. To convince Texans of his wire's efficacy, a major manufacturer named Joseph Glidden sent a crack salesman, Warren Gates, to San Antonio, where he had a corral built on the central Military Plaza using Glidden wire. Gates then hired cowboys to go out and round up some of the biggest, meanest longhorns they could find. Meanwhile he was circulating through town promoting the planned demonstration and taking bets, thereby acquiring the sobriquet "Bet-A-Million" Gates. The cowboys returned, driving the cattle into the corral. A sizable, skeptical crowd pressed to see as the ornery beasts wheeled around and prepared to break out. Coming up against the wire, they attempted to force their way through despite the damage to their hide, but the wire and the posts held firm. Again and again the angered animals hurled themselves against the obstruction until finally, baffled and bleeding, they stopped. At which point Gates had the cowboys get on top of the fence and wave their saddle blankets, starting the action anew. This went on through the night, the scene illuminated by torches. When finally, the next day, the longhorns gave up, exhausted, one post had been broken, but the wire remained intact.

San Antonio immediately went on a barbed wire-buying spree, and the rest of Texas followed.

The earliest strand of barbed wire in Smith's collection comes from Persia and is unlike any other, being made of camel's hair and thorns. The kind we are familiar with had its origins in the American Plains states where several individuals in the same year, 1867, took out patents. The fact that designs for the wire were patentable accounts for their multiplicity: each patent holder hoped to capture the market with something perceived as more desirable than competing styles. That market was a rich one, growing initially out of farmers' needs to keep free-ranging cattle out of their fields. Later, ranchers wanted to restrict their cattle to specific areas for control of breeding and other purposes.

Before farmers and ranchers came to an accommodation, there were feuds and often bloody battles between those who tilled the soil and those whose livestock roamed it. Other battles were fought in the courts over questions of patent infringement as manufacturers copied designs without a by-your-leave.

Give or take a handful, there seem to have been about a thousand variations, in one-, two-, and three-strand wire. Prickette owns between 400 and 500, while Smith figures he has around 650. Some are thin, some wide like ribbon. All are collected in a standard length, 18 inches, the reason being that in some instances barbs were used sparingly, with as much as a linear foot between.

Prickette keeps part of his collection in his office in Waco; the rest is stored at home. He has also contributed enough to Waco's Homer Garrison Museum and Texas Ranger Hall of Fame for impressive exhibits. On long-term loan to the University of Texas Institute of Texan Cultures in San Antonio is Prickette's walking stick made of barbed wire. Approximately 100 years old, this was a promotional gimmick put out by a leading wire manufacturer. One can imagine the popularity of such lethal walking sticks among nervous denizens of today's crime-ridden cities if some smart operator were to bring them back.

Smith's collection is divided between his house and barn. In the house's foyer one wall is occupied by a round board about the size of a wagon wheel on which specimens of wire radiate, spoke-like, from a hub. Each is labeled, with name, patent number and date—if there was a patent. Current prices among collectors also are listed, ranging from ten cents to four hundred dollars. The rarest wires are grouped together. Ironically, rarity results from a wire being a poor seller and thus being discontinued after a short run.

The barn has room for three more wheels, a series of panels and some cases on the floor—all holding wire. Smith points out an especially vicious wire intended to discourage depredations by buffaloes. A modern import from the Netherlands is a yellow plastic ribbon with steel points in it—practical but for some reason not popular in this country. One three-paneled screen displays a collection separate from Frank Smith's. Violet Smith, too, collects barbed wire; the fever apparently is catching.

Together, the couple have collected soil samples from each of Texas' 254 counties, many of which they visited specially for this purpose. A number of the samples were acquired during hunting trips to West Texas. All of them, in little plastic containers, are mounted in the living room on a wall map of the state. Frank also collects tools used in connection with stringing or cutting barbed wire and installing fence posts.

Although for Prickette, with his full-time county job, collecting is a hobby, for Frank Smith in retirement it has become a way of life—one in which practically every day holds the possibility of an exciting new find.

PERSONAL and PUBLIC

Everything Except Queen Victoria's Bloomers

Although he claims to be retired, Elton M. Hyder, Jr. still keeps his impressive corner office in the Fort Worth law firm he headed. Perhaps he needs it as a place to store the overflow from his collection at home. Both residence and office are large, and scarcely an inch of unoccupied surface is visible in either.

Hyder, a graduate of the University of Texas Law School in Austin, was admitted to the bar in 1943. Lawyers and professors run in the family. His father, who had come as a flyer to Fort Worth, a World War I military aviation center, practiced law before him. His elder son is a lawyer in his firm; the younger, a professor.

Within a few years of starting practice Hyder had published a book on oil and gas law and found himself attached to the legal team that condemned General Hideki Tojo to death as a World War II criminal. The first object he ever collected was picked up in Tokyo in 1946 for a dollar; a Buddha. More Buddhas followed.

The person who influenced his becoming a real collector was Roscoe Pound, dean of the Harvard Law School, who, having had the resources during the Great Depression, bought up paintings of English jurists. Hyder, a special student at Harvard in 1949-1950 when he was thinking of becoming a professor, was motivated to do likewise. (He has given the law school in Austin some 2,000 such works.) He went on to acquire in many other areas and continues to buy freely, even compulsively, with certain apparent predilections but few restrictions.

A visitor to the office is introduced to a young woman, just arrived from Austin where she has been uncrating and identifying the contents of a shipment from England. These are destined to become gifts to the university, joining the paintings, six floors of books and documents donated to the law library, and a collection of posters from the First World War now reposing on campus in the Harry Ransom Humanities Research Center. The young woman describes the current haul to the extent that she has been able to explore it so far: two dozen oil portraits, chief among them Henry VIII; a lectern, a settee, chests, wood panels decorated with biblical scenes; a Bible box, a lidded storage bench; pikes, spears, portrait lithographs, theater prints (a special interest of Mrs. Hyder); a snuff box in the shape of a boar's head; and specimens of rare seventeenth-century stumpwork, a kind of needlework in which all or

A formal Greek stoa was added to the 1916 Tudor mansion that houses the vast collections of Martha and Elton Hyder of Fort Worth.

Royal Russian crowns make a
unique centerpiece on a Georgian
table opulently set with continental
silver and gold tableware.

141

most of the ornament is raised into relief on a foundation of wool or cotton-wool.

If one were to list the contents of Hyder's office unrelated to the practice of law, the tally would have to take account of Remington cowboy bronzes, Fabergé bronzes of mounted charging Cossacks (something that occupied the master before he turned to jewelry and gem-studded eggs), carved African tribal figures, nineteenth-century English paintings, an antique rosewood chair and other pieces of period furniture, elaborate clocks, pistols, daggers, brocades, and many other items.

Now, multiply the foregoing twentyfold, add other unusual and unique items such as a Chagall canvas, a Rembrandt etching, and a wall of exceptional icons, mainly Russian, and one begins to get some idea of the scene in the Hyder mansion. For it truly is one, in Southern plantation style. The host will greet you wearing Bermuda shorts, a garb he prefers for most occasions. He may maintain a joking patter as he shows guests around, but it is clear that his possessions are dear to him. And when he parts with something, it is for a purpose. His presentation to his alma mater of what constitutes virtually a whole law library was intended to increase young people's awareness of "the majesty of the law."

There is a central staircase across the hall as one enters the house, and glowering down from the landing is a fierce carved African with a spear. Flanked by foliage, he could almost be on home territory. To the right is the living room. Hyder gestures toward an Italianate painting of the Madonna. "Amon Carter sold me that." (A surprise to one who has been led to believe that Carter, treated elsewhere in this book, owned nothing but Western art.) "Now, these invitations," indicating them on a table, "were sent out for the wedding of the Dauphin of France." The time was the early 1700s, which would make him the son of Louis XIV.

Another table holds a pair of what seem to be sculpted rams' heads. It turns out they are actual rams' heads, preserved. Scottish regiments utilized rams as mascots, with unfortunate results for the favored animals which, in World War I, were sent ahead of the troops. "And of course," says Hyder, "mowed down by German machine guns."

Fabergé Cossacks, like those in the office, provide dramatic accents. Probably not all are on display; Hyder owns some 35 of the bronzes. He picks up a delicately painted fan. "This was Consuelo Vanderbilt's when she made her debut in society." It develops that the original owner of the fan, after an unsuccessful marriage or two, took a famous French aviator as husband. They lived in a "romantic" villa outside Paris. At one point the Hyders were approached to buy the villa, but that was one thing they apparently were able to get along without.

A jeweled crown presented to the Czar and Czarina by their royal regiment stands on a small cushion. The jewels, it turns out, are of industrial quality, but the crown glitters nonetheless. Other gems, precious and semi-precious, in a variety of settings are from the personal collection of Hyder's favorite contemporary jeweler Kenneth Lane, who sold them when closing his London flat some time ago. (Lane had been a dinner guest of the Hyders a few nights earlier. And a recent house guest was the manager of Claridges. The Hyders' assemblage of friends is as diverse and impressive as their objets d'art.)

"It took me 25 years to get this," Hyder says. "This" is a purse owned by a chancellor of England under Queen Victoria (vide its monogram, "V.R.") Hyder owns eight such purses from different periods. England itself, he notes, has only four. "I'm trying to buy one now—from the chancellor under Elizabeth."

A regretful aside: "I nearly got Queen Victoria's bloomers in an auction but Malcolm Forbes topped me. He has them in his apartment in London."

There are two elegant champagne buckets from the old German ocean liner *Bremen*, and on another table half a dozen choice pieces from a collection of derringers, the

An amalgam of treasures from one end of the earth to the other are arranged in effusive still lifes.

Every surface in the Hyder mansion is encrusted with a diverse representation of the couple's wide-ranging collecting interests.

Left: Draped in Hungarian embroidered cloth, a round table in the living room holds Russian bronzes and Persian jeweled boxes.

A colorful collection of antique Russian papier-mache eggs figures among the keepsakes assembled on the creamy Siena marble in Martha Hyder's dressing room.

short-barreled, big-bored pistols so important in the taming of the West. They are not missed from a well-stocked room elsewhere in the house devoted exclusively to firearms.

Grouped on a section of wall are sketches of French theater costumes and Russian designs for ballet and opera sets. There is also a series of paintings on glass, a form of naive art produced in India for sale to the ruling British.

Hyder picks up a knife—the hunting knife of the luckless Archduke Ferdinand of Austria whose assassination, with that of his wife Sophia, sparked the First World War.

A particular prize is a family album. The family was Lord Randolph Churchill's, and the star, of course, is Winston, from childhood into youth.

At the end of the leisurely, instructive stroll through the house, Hyder sums up with a simple statement that seems beyond challenge: "Every day we have things coming in."

No doubt, had he been in Austin some days later to show the visitor through the Tarlton Law Library, Hyder could have made the same statement. The library, in a handsome six-story structure at the University of Texas, opened in 1980 and ranks as the nation's largest in its field under one roof. As one of the wealthiest of the law school's alumni, Hyder has made the building the repository of thousands of objects, many related to juridical history. His wife, Martha Rowan Hyder, is credited with using her own inherited money (her father headed Rowan Drilling Company) to augment his purchases. (Hyder has commented that she "has a black belt in buying.") She also masterminds the disposition of the objects throughout the six floors and decides on the accompanying touches. Between them the couple have created something unprecedented among law libraries.

The Hyder presence is inescapable from the moment one walks into the lobby ringed with portrait paintings of past legal luminaries. These hang above antique tables and flower-filled vases. Each item on display carries identification as a gift of Elton Hyder.

From floor to floor there are few expanses of wall where something bespeaking the Hyder bounty is not to be seen. The first barrister to sit for his portrait is represented by the portrait, a large one: big buckles on his shoes and trousers, a red ribbon tied around his legal briefs. Such red ribbons are still to be seen in the Inns of Court today. More portraits abound, as do engravings and drawings of courtroom activity and legal documents on paper, parchment, and vellum. Arranged along the halls are choice pieces of furniture, some from old courts of law. It is possible, from certain of these specimens to trace phases in the evolution of chairs. First there were benches with lidded seats, providing opportunity in the closet-poor Middle

Ages for storage beneath. Gradually, benches acquired arms and backs. Thrones and throne-like chairs developed, storage space often being eliminated. The majesty of the law was upheld with ever more dignified underpinnings. Such continuity is stressed in various strands of the Hyders' collection.

There are desks, tables, cabinets, tapestries—mostly antique European—a lawyer's shingle, and a barrister's wig. There are African baskets too, and much else that seems to have little or no thematic connection with the collection as a whole. For example, a suit of chain mail from the time of the Crusaders, pieces of English stumpwork, a display of World War I posters. There are carved American eagles, quilts, folk artifacts, portraits of U.S. presidents.

A great deal of what has been contributed by the Hyders is utilitarian as well as luxurious, dedicated to providing physical comfort and convenience for students. A roomful of computers has red walls, painted at Mrs. Hyder's direction to complement the green of the terminal screens and create a restful contrast for the eyes. Areas for reading or relaxation are fitted with inviting sofas in richly patterned Turkish-style cushions. The weary are encouraged to stretch out and put their (shoeless) feet up. Special areas have been set aside for smoking. Niches contain tables with jigsaw puzzles waiting to be assembled. Cacti of many varieties, some rare and exotic looking, are spotted about. (Students are hired by the Hyders to keep them watered.) Floors are covered with lustrous, multi-colored kilims. (When these began to lose their brilliance under fluorescent lighting, Mrs. Hyder had the university sheathe the lights.)

A routine has been established whereby, each spring, the Hyders and an entourage spend three weeks in Austin for the purpose of installing new acquisitions and rearranging what is already on the premises. The crew arrives at the library early in the evening and works in the basement until closing time at eleven. Then it takes over the building, moving furniture and pictures, hammering and painting. This goes on until morning, Mrs. Hyder often staying through the night, supervising.

The majesty of the law plus the majesty of the Hyders makes for a heady mix. Freshmen walking into Tarlton Law Library have been known to turn around and walk out, thinking they have stumbled into the wrong building.

PERSONAL and PUBLIC

Tall on the Panhandle

Turned loose behind farmer J. B. Buchanan's house about 75 miles northeast of Amarillo, near where State Highway 207 is intersected by local route 281, Don Quixote would have reason to run himself ragged. For here, like lofty sentinels—or, as the Knight of La Mancha would perceive them, monsters to be vanquished with his lance—stand a cluster of old windmills.

Actually, American windmills are of a kind indigenous to this continent. A Quixote, however, would still find them worthy albeit somewhat unfamiliar-looking antagonists. Ingeniously varied from model to model, some open up like umbrellas, others fan out into pie-shaped wedges.

If windmills seem an odd thing to collect, Buchanan, a hale octogenarian, can only plead a hopeless addiction to them dating from early childhood. A photograph taken in 1909 shows him in the background of a group dressed in Sunday best, a child of two or three on a high rung of a windmill tower, held by his father standing a couple of rungs below. In a memoir written for *Windmiller's Gazette* (Canyon, Tex.), II, No. 2 (Spring 1983), Buchanan recalls, "Like most people in this part of the good old U.S.A., the windmills attracted my attention much more than the farm work and chores attached. They played in the wind like a boy's kite.

"When I was six years old I would baby sit with my twin sisters while Mother was working with my Dad, and in return she would write for windmill literature for me to look at. While an early teenager I mounted an old discarded metal Fairbanks Morse windmill on Dad's high gate post. This mill was patented in 1897. It got a lot of attention, especially from the puzzled, thirsty cattle."

A combination of factors contributed to the decline in the use and manufacture of windmills. The railroads, which had stationed the devices at intervals along the tracks to draw up water for the boilers of steam engines, converted to diesel fuel. Electric power became available to pump water to farms and households and also to mill grain; and many growing communities invested in municipal water systems. A heavy blow was struck in World War II when the metal that had largely replaced wood in windmill construction was needed for defense.

Buchanan felt a compulsion to rescue and preserve examples of the vanishing windmill, without which whole areas of the West could scarcely have supported human

Behind farmer J.B. Buchanan's house in the Texas
Panhandle stands an army of windmills, like
sentinels on the prairie.

and domestic animal life as early as they did. He found a few windmills that still were intact but, more often, he had to scour the length and breadth of Texas and neighboring states for missing parts. Following 100 leads to locate a single part was nothing unusual. Today, besides what is standing on his property, this assiduous tracker has a couple of mills in his barn in the process of being rebuilt.

While claiming no favorites among brands in his collection, Buchanan acknowleges a special affection for Eclipses—having, as he says, "been raised under an old wooden Eclipse." The railroads, too, used these in a special outsized model. In pioneer days many ranchers made a point of having an Eclipse as their basic workhorse, with something called a Star to take over in the event of emergency.

Although windmills differ in details, all are constructed to reduce resistance to high winds (by slats opening up after the fashion of venetian blinds, for example.) Otherwise, the wheels might be shattered or blown off. Tails and oftentimes ornamental weights also determine appropriate responses to breeze or gale. But when winds hit 90 miles per hour, nothing is safe. Such a wind once broke the wheel shaft and some of the wooden fans of a railroad-type Eclipse Buchanan had painstakingly assembled. Nothing would do but that he rebuild the 18-foot wheel, and about a year later it was again ready to mount on its tower. Buchanan was so eager to see the job finished that instead of waiting for the big rig that had put it up in the first place, he hired a smaller one. The means were unequal to the end: the wheel was dropped as it was being lowered, and the tail that had survived the windstorm broke. Again he had a repair job on his hands but, as he writes in the *Windmiller's Gazette*, "this time I waited until the big rig could come to raise it up."

Buchanan's windmills are not operative today in the sense of powering pumps. The excellence of the collection is so widely recognized, however, that, on two occasions when the Smithsonian Institution in Washington, D.C. wished to acquire antique windmills to add to the permanent exhibition in its American History Museum, it turned to Buchanan. Each time, although reluctant to part, first, with a twelve-foot Eclipse, then a ten-foot Standard, he acceded to the request. The Eclipse is kept turning by an electric motor. Buchanan enjoys quoting the words on a plaque at its base, a familiar adage in his area: "No woman should live in this country who cannot climb a windmill or shoot a gun."

Climbing a tower can be a scary business, and Buchanan has tales to tell on the subject. One concerns an exceptionally tall tower—132 feet, to be exact. The cowboys employed by the owner were supposed to take turns climbing to the top when anything had to be repaired, but most of them simply quit their jobs. One man who was terrified but couldn't afford to quit was repeatedly saved by his wife, who, when his turn came, always washed another cowboys' clothes in exchange for his services as pinch hitter. In another case a farmer climbing his own tower made the mistake of looking up at the sky. Moving clouds created the illusion that the tower was falling, so the poor fellow jumped. "He couldn't hardly walk the rest of his life," says Buchanan.

A payoff in personal satisfaction for cooperating with the Smithsonian came when Buchanan and his wife visited Washington in August 1981. They went to see both windmills, then—a particular thrill—had the Standard pointed out to them on a bus tour as a sight of special interest that could be glimpsed through the window of the museum's bookshop on Constitution Avenue.

Pieces of the Raymond and Patsy Nasher sculpture collection are shared with the public at NorthPark Center, a shopping mall in Dallas owned by Nasher.

PERSONAL and PUBLIC

"Eventually Dallas Caught Up"

Art is like air to Raymond D. and Patsy Nasher of Dallas. It surrounds them at home, indoors and out. Not far from where they live, NorthPark National Bank, headed by Nasher, is a showcase for art. The shopping center he owns in which the bank is located provides a public setting for sculpture on loan from the couple's personal collection.

How the Nashers built up the collection, one of the finest of modern sculpture in the Southwest, if not the entire country, is a story that goes back some 30 years. In the late 1950s Patsy saw a Jean Arp she thought would make a fine birthday present for her husband, but at the last minute she wavered and had him take a look at it before writing out a check. They continued for some time acquiring on a relatively modest scale, buying what they liked, without any real idea of how far their shared interest would carry them.

Actually, their first art purchase took place in 1951, two years after they had met and married in Boston. A Ben Shahn gouache in a New York gallery caught their fancy and ended up on their wall. It was after they had moved to Dallas, and when Nasher was developing NorthPark Shopping Center, with its built-in plan for display of sculpture, that they made this form of art their prime concern. Over the years, becoming more secure in their taste and easier about spending large sums of money, they have surrounded themselves with treasures of sufficient quality and variety to provide the basis for museum exhibits. In April 1987 the Dallas Museum of Art mounted a major one, which later traveled to the National Gallery of Art in Washington.

The couple's education in art has been gained mainly in the process of looking, studying, and acquiring. College did not prepare them for connoisseurship: his major was political science; hers, American studies. He has since returned to the academic scene as a visiting professor in the graduate school of education at Harvard and visiting fellow and professor at the University of Massachusetts. Those who remember the two of them in the days when they were just starting to collect recall that Mrs. Nasher would fly from Dallas to New York four times a year—twice in the spring, twice in the fall—to see what was new in the galleries. She liked to make these trips with a woman friend now deceased, Shaindy Fenton of Fort Worth, who as a dealer and an experienced collector of contemporary art

153

could point a beginner toward the right choices.

Patsy now has "a fabulous eye," according to her husband. But he and she differ somewhat in what most attracts them. She is on record as favoring small objects such as weavings, pre-Columbian figurines, and antiquities, while he likes it "all out where I can see it. I'm interested in art that's related to public spaces," he says. "It's difficult for most people to go to art. Art should be a part of the physical environment and go to them."

The Nashers discontinued their pre-Columbian collecting when he served on the UNESCO commission of the United Nations and that group established a covenant prohibiting the removal of national treasures from their country of origin. Some of the weavings cherished by Mrs. Nasher, of a quality that might earn them the rating of Guatemalan national treasures, are displayed in the Dallas museum, to which they have been promised as gifts.

The Nasher home in North Dallas is comfortable, clean-lined, not grand. Designed by a local architect, Howard Meyer, in the spirit of Frank Lloyd Wright, it seems to grow naturally out of its setting of lawns ringed by woods. A long window wall in the living room offers a sweeping view of sculpture outside. Inside, a powerful Picasso canvas from 1970, *Man and Woman*, said to express the painter's recognition of the inevitability of his own death, dominates one end of the room. The opposite end is given over to Giacometti: a painting above the fireplace flanked by two elongated sculptures, a chariot with driver and a woman. On a glass-topped table and elsewhere are smaller sculptures by Matisse, Archipenko, Beuys, Lipchitz, and a maquette by Willem de Kooning.

In the adjoining room, a plaster of the famous Brancusi *The Kiss*, at once simple and sophisticated, rests on the dining table. A commanding presence on the floor, standing taller than a man, is a whimsical Claes Oldenberg *Typewriter Eraser* made of stainless steel, aluminum, and ferro cement. There are also sculptures by Roy Lichtenstein, two by Picasso, and, among the paintings, another Picasso, a double portrait by Andy Warhol of Patsy with a daughter, and abstractions by Morris Louis and Hans Hoffman.

Pre-Columbian pieces line a hallway. But in the last analysis it is the sculpture, ranging from Rodin's day to the present, that creates this collection's special impact. A partial roster includes Calder, Moore, Caro, Miró, Maillol, Arp, Noguchi, Tony Smith, David Smith, Beverly Pepper, Serra, Ernst, Lipchitz, Di Suvero, Hepworth, Newman, and Dubuffet. The largest pieces are outside, spaced around the grounds.

Many of the sculptures have anecdotes to go with them—the how, when, and where of their acquisition.

Having decided they needed a major piece by either Henry Moore or Barbara Hepworth, the Nashers attended a Hepworth exhibition at London's Tate Gallery and settled on the biggest work in the show. It turned out that the artist had promised it to Cambridge University on loan, but that difficulty was resolved when the university agreed to accept another, less monumental Hepworth instead.

Getting the Hepworth should have satisfied the Nashers' demand for something by one of the two great British sculptors. Their desire for a Moore, however, persisted and led them to the artist's studio in Much Haddam, Hertfordshire, England. Having read a profile of him in *The New Yorker*, they knew there was a private studio in addition to the one he had shown them, so they asked for a look at that. Here they saw a three- or four-inch model of what was to be the first in a large "Vertebrae" series and were immediately taken with it. Moore promised them a chance to buy one if he produced a finished version. They also admired a *Reclining Figure No. 9*, which was nearing completion, and agreed that it would satisfy them in the event he stopped work on the "Vertebrae."

What actually happened some time later was that Moore's dealer called to alert them to the opening of the next Moore show, at the Tate. Both the works in which they had expressed interest were to be on display; if they still intended to buy one they'd better hurry over. They lost no time catching a plane, and once at the museum found themselves torn between the two, both of which looked wonderful. Unable to make up their minds, they did something that, according to the startled artist, no collector had

Above: A plaster of the famous Brancusi The Kiss *rests on the Nasher's dining table. Right:* Five Hammering Men *by Jonathan Borofsky; wood, steel, paint and motor; 14½' high; 1982.*

154

155

ever done before: purchased two major Moores. The Nashers were equally startled. On the way home they began to wonder if they had overextended themselves.

Evidently not, in view of the pace at which they have gone on collecting. What they did come to realize about Henry Moore, however, was that it was easier to have his works shipped to Dallas than to have a particular one transported from their garden to the NorthPark center for the benefit of shoppers. Along with other sculptures by Barbara Hepworth and Alexander Calder, it turned out to be too heavy for the movers to handle. Fortunately, there are other Moores that the Nashers have been able to lend to the mall.

From the time Nasher started planning the NorthPark Shopping Center in the early sixties, his idea was to incorporate art into it as an integral element. His bank that is part of the center was designed by architects instructed to create a quiet, relaxed environment in which the graphics and sculpture rather than the building itself would provide dramatic interest. The bank's own collection is drawn upon for exhibits in the vaulted lobby. One memorable exhibit that attracted the gaze toward the ceiling with strong, ebullient color consisted of a dozen multimedia images by Frank Stella, *Illustrations After El Lissitzky's Had Gadya*. Completed in late 1984, these were inspired by a series of illustrations done by an early-twentieth-century Russian artist for the "Had Gadya," a parable nursery rhyme (much like "The House That Jack Built") that comes at the end of the Jewish Haggadah, or Passover, service. The titles of the sequence convey the gist of the rhyme: "One small Goat Papa Bought for Two Zuzin," "A Hungry Cat Ate Up the Goat," "Then Came a Dog and Bit the Cat," "Then Came a Stick and Beat the Dog," and so on. Stella has captured the liveliness and naive charm of the singsong story, not realistically but in joyous forms and colors. Ranged round the lobby high overhead, the images welcome visitors into the bank like a fanfare.

Each one is composed of a background sheet and a shaped collage sheet. The background sheets are hand painted and then printed with several colors. The collage sheets are printed in multiple runs of colors from silkscreens, linoleum blocks, and lithographic plates. Production was by Stella assisted by three printers in his own New York printing studio.

Visitors with or without business to transact are encouraged to view the art on the bank's upper floors, but since private offices and the conference room where the board meets are not routinely open to the casual browser, some major treats may be missed except during a guided tour. It would be a particular pity not to get a look at the conference room. A large wood-paneled oval, it is hung all around with prints from Matisse's *Jazz* series. Anyone who

The wood-paneled conference room at NorthPark Bank, also owned by Nasher, is hung with Henri Matisse's Jazz Series, 1947.

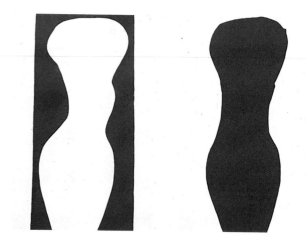

156

has seen these same prints in a beautiful book published several years ago knows their vividness and *joie de vivre*. The book, however, does not prepare one for the impact of these 20 gorgeous collages even more vibrantly re-created in larger format.

Besides the Matisses, there are other silkscreens or lithographs by the likes of the up-and-coming Jean-Michel Basquiat, Alan Cote, Richard Estes, Jasper Johns, Motherwell, Calder, Oldenberg, Lichtenstein, Warhol, and, again, Stella. The last is further represented by a tapestry and by a mixed-media work on aluminum and fiberglass, *Diepholz II*, 1982, one of a series depicting racetracks, with which Stella is fascinated. Calder, Dine, and Gottlieb also have tapestries in the collection.

Thoroughly at home in NorthPark's bastion of the modern and experimental are New Guinean, Native American, and pre-Columbian artifacts and African sculptures.

The Nashers' personal collection of sculpture yields important loans to the bank as well as to the shopping center. Likely to be encountered in the bank are pieces by Robert Adams, Charles Arnoldi, Sergio Camargo, Alain Kirili, Martin Puryear, and James Surls.

In the 1960s, when the Nashers started sharing larger works with the community by placing them in the shopping center, the community as a whole did not seem favorably impressed. In the words of the bank's executive vice president Dale R. Terry, the Texas definition of art at that time was bluebonnets and cowboys. (The bluebonnet school, so-called after the state flower and stressing the bucolic, still has many practitioners and admirers. And the cowboy, too, though a vanishing breed, remains a formidable figure in the art of the people.) "We stayed on course," Terry recalls with satisfaction, "and eventually Dallas caught up."

Permanent installations in the shopping center include a series of Cor-ten wedges by Beverly Pepper, *Dallas Land Canal*, at its south entrance; also a pair of large works by Jonathan Borofsky, one inside the mall titled *Hammering Men* and a companion piece, *Hammering Man*, on the outside. Both are motorized for movement. The first is a group of five tall figures, flat like cut-outs, raising and lowering their arms, wielding hammers; in the second, the act is being performed by a solitary individual. These are not icons to cozy up to; in fact they are rather sinister. Although people walk by them without a second glance, obviously accustomed to them, one wonders to what extent the ordinary citizen really likes them. It wasn't so long ago that the Nashers lent the bank their Claes Oldenberg sculpture, the giant *Typewriter Eraser*. The word that went around then was that they were trying to erase their big mistakes.

The way of the benefactor isn't always easy.

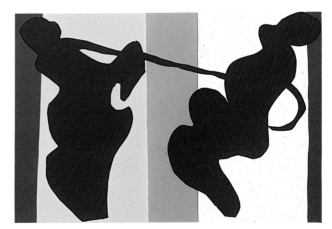

PRO BONO PUBLICO

PRO BONO PUBLICO

Cadillac Ranch:
Art (?) as Surprise

Do ten tail-finned Cadillacs constitute a collection? In any other state but Texas they probably would. Perhaps the fact that they are claimed by their owner, Stanley Marsh 3, to be making an artistic statement should give them the standing of a collection in Texas, too.

The ten cars, ranging in vintage from 1949 to 1963, were buried front ends first, rear ends protruding, at intervals along a straight line in an alfalfa field beside Interstate 40 just west of Amarillo. The angle of burial, make of it what you will, is supposed to be that of the Great Pyramid of Egypt. Since the planting in 1974, urban sprawl has overtaken the site, which originally was out in the country but now is hard to spot among the trailer parks and motels.

Asked about it shortly before the tenth anniversary of its creation, Marsh, who owns the land and a lot more besides, responded by expounding his theory of art to *Dallas Morning News* reporter Bill Minutaglio: "The most significant art is the art we never see. The art we dream about. When I saw the *Mona Lisa*, I was disappointed. See, I like art that comes as an abrupt surprise. Art that's not in a museum, that's not on a wall. I like being able to make up my own mind what art is. I am building up a system of unanticipated rewards. Take Cadillac Ranch. It's not for people who know about it. It's for the guy who is driving in from Tucumcari [New Mexico], his kids are crying, the air conditioning isn't working, his wife is upset and then all of a sudden, there it is. The guy's gonna say, 'Honey, what are those cars doing over there?' Then those people can use their critical faculties to judge whether they like it or not.

"I hope they like it. I want people to like it. I want to be popular."

Cadillac Ranch was the idea of three members of an avant-garde California artists group, the Ant Farm: Hudson Marquez, Doug Michels, and Chip Lord. Securing Marsh's backing, they spent six weeks scouring the Panhandle for cars of the right vintage and style. The cost for all ten came to less then $4000. Not only were these automotive behemoths long out of date, but in the era of the energy crisis they seemed particularly, and pathetically, anachronistic—probably the point of the Ant Farm's exercise.

The wherewithal to make this point came out of the ground and the air—from natural gas and broadcasting enterprises—among other sources of Marsh's enormous wealth. He is accustomed to spending money on the unconventional and reaping publicity therefrom. His 10,000-acre ranch outside Amarillo has been home to double-humped camels, llamas, peacocks, a yak, and a two-tailed cow. He owns the "World's Largest Soft Pool Table," a plot of ground 90 feet by 180 feet, the location of which is kept secret from all but a few intimates and which is moved once or twice a year, presumably to throw possible thieves off the scent. The table comes complete with a 40-foot-long cue stick, ten giant vinyl balls and a gargantuan piece of chalk. At the edge of a local lake, jutting out over it, is something called "Amarillo Ramp," constructed for Marsh by Robert Smithson. Made of earth, it would be a good jumping-off place for a car destined for a watery grave. The jokes carry over to Marsh's office, where a stuffed tattooed pig with wings is suspended from the ceiling, an erstwhile drinking companion named Minnesota Fats.

What happens to automobiles left out of doors in all kinds of weather has happened to the Caddies: the finish has discolored and cracked, rust has attacked, and so have vandals and defacers. Autographs have been scratched on fins, shots fired through them. Once, in the middle of the night, unseen hands painted all ten cars bright red. Marsh, claiming to like the result, recommended that the same be done to spruce up the Sphinx and the Statue of Liberty.

Stanley Marsh 3's Cadillac Ranch, ten tail-finned autos planted in the Panhandle, adheres to the Texan's theory that art should be an abrupt surprise.

163

The Pate Museum of Transportation, a roadside attraction near Fort Worth since 1969, features all manner of transport, including automobiles, railroad cars, helicopters, seagoing vessels, and combat tanks.

PRO BONO PUBLICO

Collecting Movement(s)

Adlai McMillan ("Aggie") Pate, Jr. is disarmingly frank about why he collects classic cars, airplanes, bejeweled watches, and other expensive items. "I loved wealth," he says, "and the things you could do with wealth. And I liked the big Packards and the big Cadillacs."

When he started collecting, he didn't have much to spend; but things were cheap then. He bought his first car, a V-16 Caddy with 140,000 miles on it, for $250. "I bought that pretty Packard that you saw for $250," he says, "and drove it from Phoenix in here."

"In here" is Fort Worth, where the Pate Museum of Transportation has been a roadside attraction, on U.S. Highway 377, since August 1969.

"And we bought a Rolls Royce for $1,400," Pate continues. "I always wanted a private airplane and a private rail car and I couldn't afford either one. But I managed to get one (a railroad car) to look at." "Sunshine Special's Ellsmere," as this is known, was built in 1914 by the Wagner Palace Car Company for Dr. William Seward Webb of St. Albans, Vermont. Earlier, Dr. Webb had had "Sunshine Special's" predecessor "Ellsmere I" built as a wedding present for his bride, Eliza Osgood Vanderbilt. An almost foreordained gift, it would seem, since Miss Vanderbilt came from a family whose vast fortune was founded on railroads, and Webb, besides being a surgeon, was president of the Wagner Palace Car Company. The couple took their honeymoon aboard "Ellsmere I." Then, in 1889, it became part of an all-private train on which the Webbs with their three children, four guests, a staff of Pinkerton detectives, a military guard, a complement of railroad employees, a lady's maid, two nurses, and eight porters embarked on a 6,000-mile hunting expedition, from New York to San Francisco and back.

The successor, "Sunshine Special's Ellsmere," possibly even more elegant in its fittings, paneling, and furnishings, achieved its moment of glory in 1932. On a New York-to-Chicago run setting a new rail passenger speed record, it was the rear car of the 20th Century Limited of the New York Central line. Dr. Webb had sold it by then, and his Wagner Palace Car Company had been absorbed by Pullman.

In subsequent years "Sunshine Special's Ellsmere" underwent modernization and was used by various railroad executives in the conduct of their business. Finally, in 1961, it was retired from service, whereupon Pate saw his opportunity and wangled it as a gift for the Fort Worth Children's Museum (later the Fort Worth Museum of Science & History), of which he was president. Pate's father and a partner had established the Texas Refinery Corp., which owned the Texas Refinery Recreation Ranch, and it was there that "Sunshine Special's Ellsmere" ended up on a siding, and the children and their parents came to see it. Once again it was refurbished, having been given permanent plumbing, electricity, and new air conditioning. In 1970 the Fort Worth Museum of Science & History voted to cede ownership of the car to The Pate Foundation, a family enterprise of which Aggie is president and his brother, Sebert, executive vice president. By then the Pate Museum of Transportation, supported entirely by the foundation, had come into being on the site of the Texas Refinery Recreation Ranch, and "Sunshine Special's Ellsmere," staying where it was, constituted one of the museum's biggest draws.

Other attractions are an MSB-5 mine sweeper, one of the few seagoing vessels exhibited by an inland museum; a Navy F9F "Cougar" jet, with wings folded for storage on an aircraft carrier; an F-86 "Sabre" jet; three military helicopters; a Korean combat tank; a London double-decker bus; a 1903 Cadillac Tonneau, the museum's oldest automobile; a fully restored 1929 Packard seven passenger, dual-windshield Phaeton featuring a custom body designed by Raymond Dietrich (this car has won first place in Classic Car Club and Antique Car Club competitions); a 1,500-volume transportation library, and more.

The grounds of the transportation museum provide the setting each spring for the Pate Swap Meet, where automobiles and auto parts change hands. Attended by approximately 4,200 antique car enthusiasts, it is the nation's third-largest get-together of its kind, topped only by those in Hershey and Carlisle, Pennsylvania.

The museum attracts visitors from all over the world, approximately 200,000 annually. Bell Helicopter regularly brings European trainees to view and study the displays.

In his office at Texas Refinery, Aggie Pate, recalling the start of the museum, says, "At first we were going to call it Gasoline Alley. I had a very close relationship with Skeezicks. You know, that's one of the few comic strips where the characters grow. Skeezicks had his sixty-fifth birthday on February 14, 1986. I had my sixty-fifth birthday that year on January 25. We're even closer in age than that; I think we're identical. He was an orphan, an abandoned baby left on Uncle Walt's doorstep February 14, 1921—Valentine's Day. Supposedly he was three weeks old. So that would put him about January 25.

"Gasoline Alley was also the pit stop for the Indianapolis 500, so it had a lot of significance for cars. But before we ever opened to the public I had a private rail car and a DC-3, so we decided to make it all kinds of transportation."

Underlying the whole concept was the idea of fuel as the motivating force, and that tied the museum to the Pate family business.

Almost as important to Pate as the museum is his watch collection. Visitors to his office are likely to have case after case of watches brought out for inspection. All are Patek Philippes, "the world's finest watch," according to their owner. When interviewed, Pate had 114.

"This one is full enamel front and back," he explains. "I bought it in 1965. Pretty, isn't it? It has a value of about $25,000. It took one man a year to make. . . . Here's something from 1850 or something like that, a presentation piece. Isn't it beautiful?"

Pointing out another, Pate says, "They have a patented electric process that turns gold a blue color. The places that haven't turned blue—where it looks like little gold flakes making a pattern—are really thin sheets of gold that have been greased to keep them from turning. It's something like tie-dying. Isn't that beautiful, though?"

Once he buys a watch, Pate never thinks of selling it. He picks more of them out of their cases where they are laid side by side. "This one cost $14,000 . . . this is $32,000 . . . this is $17,500. . . this one $25,000.

"My wife has twelve," he goes on. "She wears hers. We went to a watch show in Houston. Then we left for San

Antonio. She said, 'Well, you never did ask me, but I had one picked out I wanted.' And I said, 'Well, I didn't know we were going down there to buy anything, I thought we were just going to look.' Women don't look, you know—if it's for sale, they want it. I never did buy it. She collects Lincoln material, too."

About 20 years ago Joyce Pate developed an interest in the Great Emancipator and decided to assemble a basic Lincoln library. Pate recalls that "many a night after I had gone to bed" she would still be "poring over book catalogues. . . ." The collection was considered more or less complete by the end of 1972, when she had all the essential books and pamphlets, more than 600 of them, plus an assortment of artifacts. Among the latter are two books about Lincoln published in 1918 and 1925 for Chinese school children, a model of the railroad coach that carried the president's body from Washington to Springfield, Illinois; a black basalt bust of Lincoln from a limited edition produced by Wedgwood in 1971; and four *cartes de visite* of Mary Todd Lincoln. These *cartes* are not visiting cards despite their name but photographs of visiting-card size meant to substitute for them. Mrs. Lincoln's show her posed for Matthew Brady, wearing her inaugural gown in 1861; in 1862; in mourning after Willie's death later in 1862; and in 1863.

Their clothing is a source of pleasure for both Pates, who often order matching garb from the Hong Kong tailor who has kept Pate in three-piece business suits at a minimum rate of 25 suits a year for more than 20 years. Among their favorite his-and-hers ensembles are vivid red Western outfits made of Mexican fabric and sets of bright yellow jackets with multicolored vests in a frog and dragonfly pattern. When they're not dressing twin style, the couple take pains to wear clothes that harmonize with each other.

The oil bust had not yet struck Texas when Pate, showing off his watches, delivered himself of a surprisingly uncharacteristic remark. "I have quit buying Pateks," he said. "They've gotten so high."

PRO BONO PUBLICO

Winedale, Henkel Square, and the Dallas Museum's Bybee Collection

Whether by design or happenstance, Winedale and Henkel Square complement each other. Situated within neighborly distance in rolling country midway between Houston and San Antonio, the two restorations dovetail. The buildings of both are from the period of German and Anglo-American settlement, and their furniture and decorative and utilitarian objects all give a vivid sense of what pioneer existence was like in nineteenth-century Fayette County.

Winedale is a community more or less created by Ima Hogg; Henkel Square at Round Top is the equivalent project of Charles L. and Faith Bybee. Although Miss Hogg and Mrs. Bybee's banker-husband are both dead, Winedale continues to be maintained under the auspices of the University of Texas at nearby Austin, while the octogenarian widow carries on her work of re-creation under the auspices of the Texas Pioneer Arts Foundation, established by the Bybees in 1967. There is always enough going on at Henkel Square to keep a crew of stonemasons, carpenters, painters, a handyman, and a furniture restorer fully occupied. The public is welcomed at both locations.

The Bybees and Miss Ima, as she was known, were friends in Houston. On one occasion the trio drove out to the country together to look at a Greek Revival house in Washington-on-the-Brazos, a few miles from Round Top. The Bybees were in the market for a weekend place, and the fact that the house needed a lot of repairs didn't stop them from buying it. Having already filled their elegant Houston house with fine early-American pieces, the Bybees decided to furnish this country retreat in indigenous style. "I hadn't even heard of Texas furniture then," Mrs. Bybee says, but her researches into what went naturally with the newly acquired house soon acquainted her with its characteristics. She learned that it derived chiefly from two sources: American Empire, popular in the mid-nineteenth century in the East; and Biedermeier, modeled on French Empire and familiar to the German immigrants. Miss Ima's interest in such furniture was probably triggered at the same time.

Once they had a foothold in the area, the Bybees took advantage of other pieces of property on which stood sadly rundown houses and commercial buildings, including an apothecary's shop. They eventually had a hamlet ripe for restoration. This they named Henkel Square in honor of the man who incorporated Round Top in the 1850s, built a church for it, and served as its first mayor.

A number of the houses bore little resemblance to their original states, having been modified and then allowed to fall into disrepair. Returning them to their original sizes and shapes and disclosing their careful carpentry, the restorers allowed the simple virtues of the structures to shine once more. Their exteriors now are as they were originally, gray or white, livened with bright-colored trim.

Mrs. Bybee is knowledgeable about the houses and their construction. She explains that the earliest were likely to be one-room log cabins with lean-tos. When two of these faced each other across an enclosed passageway, the house had a so-called dog run or dog trot. In the hot Texas summer these could be—and still are—refreshingly breezy.

Spaced about Henkel Square are the apothecary shop, a one-room church-schoolhouse, clapboard and double-log houses, a weaver's cottage and a tinsmith's shop. There are 35 houses in the village and another seven on a farm nearby—approximately twice as many having been incorporated into the project since Mr. Bybee died in 1972.

Inside the buildings there are many decorative touches, relieving the sometimes roughhewn effect. Stenciled moldings and ceilings are common. Interiors of cupboards may be painted blue—the color coming from laundry blueing, which, instead of being poured out after the clothes were washed, was put to esthetic use.

Furniture found in the neighborhood and installed in the houses includes outsized dining tables for householders and their hired hands, roomy daybeds and four-posters, rockers, work tables, chairs with deerskin seats, and shipping crates spruced up with floral decorations and used for storage.

Separate from Round Top is the superb Bybee collection of classic eighteenth- and nineteenth-century American furniture. Mrs. Bybee began assembling this as a young bride with a handsome Charleston-style River Oaks house in Houston to furnish. A certain courage was called for: no one else of her acquaintance was buying that sort of thing. Even Ima Hogg, she avers, hadn't begun. Charles Bybee liked what his wife found in the New York antique shops and came to share her collector's zeal. With his enthusiastic support she attended a series of courses at Winterthur, the Delaware museum that had been the home of

Henkel Square in Central Texas is a restored community of houses and other buildings erected by the area's nineteenth-century German settlers. A project of Houstonian Faith Bybee and her late husband Charles, the structures are filled with furnishings pertinent to the pioneer existence of the Republic.

169

Americana collector Henry Francis du Pont. Eventually the Bybees had one of the most important early-American collections in the country.

In 1986, the Dallas Museum of Art—partly by purchase, partly through gift—started taking possession of the Bybee collection, valued at more than $5,000,000. The aquisition process was to be spread out over five years.

The museum is getting 98 pieces of furniture, many of them labeled with the names of their makers—a boon to scholars. These masters of their craft worked in Philadelphia, New York, Boston, Newport, Rhode Island, and Salem, Massachusetts, mainly in the eighteenth century. The emphasis is on Queen Anne pieces by New England cabinetmakers.

From such an array it is difficult to single out anything for special mention, but one might point to a distinctive, beautifully detailed Boston tall clock in burled walnut. Dating roughly from 1725–1740, this has a movement by the first known New England clockmaker, Benjamin Bagnall Sr. A Windsor-style settee from Philadelphia circa 1760–1780, combining maple, tulip poplar, and hickory woods, charms with its elegant simplicity. Another standout is a dressing table in the Queen Anne style, made of mahogany and tulip, probably in the Hartford-Wethersfield area of Connecticut between 1745–1765.

By acquiring the Bybee collection, the Dallas museum has advanced in a single step to the forefront of institutions with major holdings of American decorative art.

Almost from the beginning, Miss Ima conceived of the

Unrelated to Henkel Square except by ownership is the Bybees' superb collection of classic eighteenth- and nineteenth-century furniture by American master cabinetmakers. Now owned by the Dallas Museum of Art, the enviable Bybee Collection, with its emphasis on Queen Anne pieces by New England craftsmen—is valued at $5 million. Pictured is a pier table of mahogany, pine and tulip poplar from New York, New York, 1825–1835, maker unknown.

Boston tall clock of burled walnut; Benjamin Bagnall, Sr.; Boston, Massachusetts; 1730–1750.

High chest of drawers of walnut, maple and pine; maker unknown; Ipswich or Salem, Massachusetts; 1740–57.

Like most Southern farmhouses built in the mid-nineteenth century, the Sam Lewis house, the oldest building at the Winedale Historical Center, incorporated a substantial amount of covered open space used by the Lewis family and their slaves for eating, working and sleeping. Upper and lower galleries take advantage of breezes in the summer months.

Winedale Historical Center as a matrix for cultural studies. Shortly after she had bought the first few old houses on a farmstead in the wooded valley of Jack's Creek, she invited the University of Texas to cooperate in programs related to the complex's development. That was in 1965. Today a conference center accommodates meetings and there is an annual summer season of student Shakespeare productions in a converted barn. The students, who gather in the spring from UT campuses all over the state, live, study, rehearse, and perform at Winedale for a 14-week period.

Many more houses and buildings have been added to the initial purchase over the years, some of them being moved from other locations. Insofar as possible, old furnishings still in the area were located and returned to their original settings. By and large, the chairs, tables, beds, and wardrobes are of the types seen at Henkel Square, some of them created by the same hands. A type of wardrobe much in vogue was held together by a set of pegs which, when removed, permitted its collapse for easy transportation. Occasionally there is something unique, such as a sofa made for his own use by Christofer Friderich Carl Steinhagen, around 1860. Seven feet long, combining oak and pine, it features unusual carving with imaginative fish and swans' heads embellishing its neoclassical form. This piece remained in Steinhagen's family over the generations until Miss Ima learned of it and acquired it.

China and earthenware of the region are distributed throughout the houses. A barrel organ made in 1870 in Bohemia (now Czechoslovakia) and brought over by a settler evokes echoes of the dance hall in nearby Frelsburg as a Winedale docent cranks its handle. Programmed to play nine tunes, it starts with a reedy rendition of "The Beautiful Blue Danube," punctuated by bleeps and squeaks.

Two of the larger houses that have been restored are the McGregor-Grimm house, built in 1861, and the Lewis

house, expanded several times from the one room with loft erected by a settler from South Carolina in 1834. The entrance hall of McGregor-Grimm exhibits an ingenious decorative trick fairly common in the area: its wooden walls are painted to resemble marble. Geography and logistics accounted for this fakery. The nearest railroad station being some fifty miles distant and marble being prohibitively heavy for such a haul, even well-to-do householders were obliged to compromise when they desired marble's ultimate luxury. Stenciled and freehand wall and ceiling decorations in several rooms show a sophisticated talent and are attributed to a German immigrant, Rudolph Melchior.

When Samuel K. Lewis, a congressman of the short-lived Republic of Texas, bought the Carolina settler's house in 1848, he took advantage of its location on the stage route between Brenham and Austin to more than double its size and operate it as an inn. After Lewis's death in 1867, his family held the property until 1882. A new owner added a kitchen at the rear, replacing a separate kitchen. Gradually, however, the old building began to betray its age. Miss Ima took pity on it in 1961, and today, as the Winedale Stage Coach Inn, it is something of a showplace. No records exist indicating how the inn was furnished in Lewis's time. For the most part, the local adaptation of Biedermeier sets the tone. Painted borders on walls and on a ceiling, employing native fruit and floral motifs, have been colorfully restored, as have a realistic bowl of fruit over a fireplace and a lifelike parrot looking down from its perch on another ceiling. Again, the gifted Melchior appears to have lent his touch.

Like Miss Ima's other legacy, Bayou Bend, Winedale has continued to educate and give pleasure since her death. And as time passes, the value of its contribution as an institution dedicated to the understanding and appreciation of Texas history can only grow.

THE MUSEUM MAKERS

Ransom's Revolution

"Harry Ransom put Texas on the cultural map," wrote the late, great publisher Alfred A. Knopf in a tribute after Ransom's death in 1976. "The collections which were his pride and joy raised the university library to a distinction that ranks it with . . . the greatest in our land. And this was accomplished not in centuries but in little more than a decade."

The collections referred to are at the University of Texas, Austin, in what, in honor of its founder, is today known as the Harry Ransom Humanities Research Center.

Ransom, who spent his entire professional life at the university, rising from instructor in English to president and chancellor, conceived a new idea. It was an idea derided by some, but it worked so well that now detractors attack it for its very success.

Before Ransom's time, the collecting of books for study and criticism in a research facility had been based on the primacy of the first printed edition. It dawned on Ransom that since the first edition represented the culmination of the process whereby a book came into being, documentation of the elements leading to that point would throw light on the book's genesis and development. Such elements might include an author's notes, correspondence, drafts, revised drafts, galley proofs, corrected galley proofs, page proofs, and corrected page proofs. Personal and family papers, even if not directly related to a book, also could provide insights into the circumstances and psychological factors affecting its creation.

Original manuscripts always had been valued, but only with the establishment of the Humanities Research Center was an attempt begun to save and bring together the complete archival material of writers. Emphasis was placed on nineteenth- and twentieth-century American, British, and French authors, these being the focus of Ransom's own scholarly interest.

The opportunities for research opened by this fresh approach were enormous. Scholars soon had reason to visit and communicate with the center from every part of the globe, and do so today at the rate of about 10,000 a year. This, in fact, is a major sore point with critics, especially British, who claim they must travel thousands of miles at great expense to study their own literary past. In reply to which, Decherd Turner, director of the center until his retirement in 1988, was wont to point out that "Europe is a

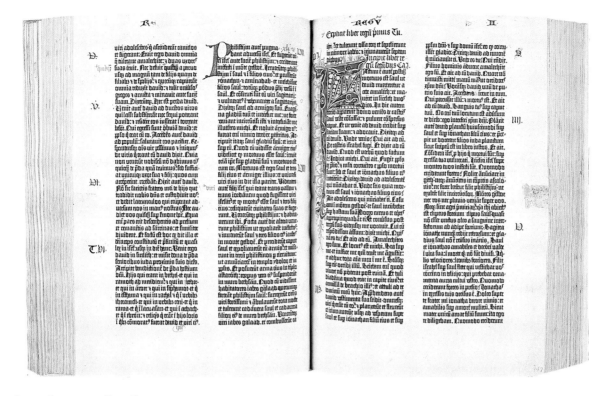

Among the treasures Harry Ransom
collected for the University of Texas'
Humanities Research Center is a Gutenberg
Bible, 1450–1455.

part of our heritage too. We have the same right as people who live in England."

The center is accommodated mainly in a large, square seven-story structure, of which it has the use of four floors, with overflow to two other buildings. At latest count it was providing space for some 9,000,000 manuscripts, 800,000 rare books, 5,000,000 photographs, an extensive theater arts collection, and 50,000 pieces of literary iconography. In this last category are paintings, drawings, photographs, and sculpltures of literary figures or subjects.

What manner of man was the innovator described by Joe B. Frantz, a historian of the West, as "the greatest single thing to happen at the University in the second third of the twentieth century?" He was, according to his widow, Hazel, who first met Harry Hunt Ransom when she enrolled in one of his freshman classes, "thoughtful, encouraging, loyal, self-effacing, unpretentious, sparkling and witty, brilliantly articulate, loving and devoted." (This description is contained in a personal communication to the author of this book. In the same letter she notes disarmingly that in a biographical sketch accompanying a col-

lection of essays by Ransom, which she edited after his death, "I have used a more objective approach.") Decherd Turner says, "As a young teacher he developed a passion for the possibilities of research in the humanities. He had this very definite idea: that he had the responsibility to change a good library system into a great one." Turner speculates that Ransom spent many sleepless nights exploring the full implications of his concept that the first printed edition is merely the end of a process. "He was laughed at," asserts Turner, "because he was a revolutionary."

Associates recall that although Ransom's personality was anything but flamboyant, he was able to generate a contagious excitement about his dreams for the center. He managed to obtain funding through the university regents rather than rely on appropriations from what he regarded as the foot-dragging state legislature. Becoming friendly with one particular book dealer who grew to share his enthusiasm and often was willing to wait to be paid, he was able to acquire collections that otherwise would have escaped for lack of ready cash. (Collections, not single volumes, were what Ransom spread his net for from the beginning. In anything pertaining to the HRC, he was a man in a hurry.)

Privately, Ransom was not much of a collector. His own library consisted essentially of the sorts of books that come into the office of a university scholar. Whatever drive he had to amass literary materials, including rare and precious works, some of them of great beauty, was channeled into collecting for the center.

And since not only what a writer has written, but what he has read, is important to an understanding of his work, the HRC has acquired a number of writers' personal libraries. Part of the library (approximately 500 volumes) accumulated by James Joyce when he was in Trieste laboring over *Ulysses* is one of them. Others include the complete libraries of Evelyn Waugh, Erle Stanley Gardner, Texas historian J. Frank Dobie, and Edward Larocque Tinker. The settings in which the three Americans did their writing have been reproduced in the center; the rooms have a Southwestern or frontier flavor. Dr. Tinker, who celebrated the exploits of the horsemen of the Americas, collected Argentinian saddles; dozens of these are displayed in his library along with other objects associated with the gauchos' way of life.

The world of publishing is represented by a room holding a part of the personal library of Alfred Knopf and his wife and copublisher, Blanche, also deceased. Many of the titles are first editions of works brought out by their distinguished house.

A suite of three rooms has been dedicated to the Texas artist and writer Tom Lea, author of *The Brave Bulls* and illustrator of books by others, including Dobie.

Among the HRC's manuscript collections, ranging from extensive to complete, are those of James Agee, Maxwell Anderson, Elizabeth Bowen, Rupert Brooke, A. E. Coppard, Gregory Corso, Thomas B. Costain, Edward Gordon Craig, Nancy Cunard, Edward Dahlberg, Arthur Conan Doyle, T. S. Eliot, William Faulkner, Graham Greene, Radclyffe Hall, Lillian Hellman, Robinson Jeffers, Oliver LaFarge, D. H. Lawrence, Sinclair Lewis, Vachel Lindsay, Carlson McCullers, Louis McNeice, John Masefield, Edgar Lee Masters, Somerset Maugham, Arthur Miller, Henry Miller, A. A. Milne, Jessica Mitford, Christopher Morley, Ogden Nash, John Cowper Powys, J. B. Priestley, Siegfried Sassoon, Anne Sexton, George Bernard Shaw,

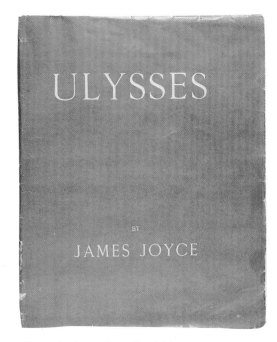

Ulysses *by James Joyce. First Edition, Shakespeare & Co., Paris, 1922.*

Edith, Osbert, and Sacheverell Sitwell, C. P. Snow, Stephen Spender, John Steinbeck, Dylan Thomas, Irving Wallace, Hugh Walpole, Jerome Weidman, Edith Wharton, Tennessee Williams, William Butler Yeats, and Louis Zukofsky.

The foregoing are all American or British. As for French authors, the HRC's archives are said to make it a resource to research into nineteenth- and twentieth-century French literature second only to the Bibliothèque Nationale in Paris.

Taking cognizance of a fairly recent renascence of fine printing and binding, the HRC devotes a special, temperature-controlled room to twentieth-century editions, many of them illustrated, constituting masterpieces of the bookmaker's art.

Conservation has come to be one of the center's chief concerns. A staff of 23 employing the most advanced techniques concentrates on the preservation of the materials held by the HRC, paying particular attention to those being borrowed for exhibition elsewhere.

In 1986 the center received one of the most impressive gifts in its history: a major portion of the nonpareil collection of rare English books and manuscripts collected by the New York investment banker Carl H. Pforzheimer, who died in 1957. These treasures had been for sale for nearly a decade, a mouth-watering temptation to individual

The frontispiece design for Lewis Carroll's Through the Looking Glass, *published in 1872, illustrates the fine art of printing.*

bibliophiles and libraries everywhere. It was H. Ross Perot, the chairman of Electronic Data Systems, of Dallas, who finally took the prize for $15 million and presented it to the university.

Already belonging to the HRC were such works as a Gutenberg Bible from 1450-1455 and a Kelmscott *Chaucer* (1896). Added through Perot's generosity were the first book ever published in English, *Recuyell of the Historyes of Troye* by Raoul Le Fevre, printed by William Caxton and Colard Mansion in 1475; the first complete Bible in English, the Coverdale Bible of 1535; three copies of the King James Bible; four folios and eighteen quartos of Shakespeare's plays, English translations of Plutarch's *Lives* (1579) and Cervantes' *Don Quixote* (1620); Ben Jonson's *Every Man in His Humour* (1601); Thomas Hobbes' *Leviathan* (1651); John Locke's *Essay Concerning Human Understanding* (1690); works of Chaucer,

Spenser, Bacon, Donne, and Milton, and a letter from Sir Walter Raleigh to his nephew, Sir John Gilbert. In all, there were more than 1,100 books and manuscripts spanning the period 1475 to 1700.

"The last major privately held collection of works representing the foundations of English culture" was the university's description of its catch in an official statement. Center director Turner credited Perot with "changing bibliographic geography" by bringing the Pforzheimer holdings to Texas.

Bibliographic geography had of course been changing ever since Harry Ransom began to put his ideas into effect nearly 30 years earlier. If the limits of such change within the range of HRC's interest may have all but been reached, it is because the institution Ransom left behind so superbly embodies his vision.

Carter and Richardson: The Vanishing West

Neither of them claimed to know much about art, but they both knew what they liked. And what they liked turned out to be the best of its kind.

Amon G. Carter was introduced in 1935 to the work of Charles Russell, the Montana cowboy artist. In spite of being publisher of the *Fort Worth Star-Telegram*, Carter was feeling the pinch of the Depression and had to borrow the money to buy nine Russell watercolors. Sid Richardson, building a fortune in oil, cattle, and land, likewise began his collecting—seven years later—with Russells. Carter, meanwhile, had discovered another interpreter of the Western scene, Frederic Remington, and was avidly purchasing his paintings, drawings, and bronze sculptures. Richardson followed a similar course as a collector.

The two were close friends and cronies in the Fort Worth Club, a bastion of upper-stratum bonhomie. Like Richardson, Carter spent fruitless years drilling for oil before his first well came in, but once the black gold started gushing he was wealthy for life. Richardson, on the other hand, gained and lost fortunes several times over; Carter often kept him afloat with loans.

What made ardent collectors of these hard-headed entrepreneurs was love of their part of the world and of a way of life captured by the artist's eye and hand before it passed into history.

Giles Amon Carter (his real name, though he disliked Giles so much he moved it to the middle, then reduced it to an initial) was born in December 1879 in a log cabin in Wise County in north central Texas. His father, a blacksmith and farmer, finished building a log cabin too late in the season to fill in the chinks before the freezing weather arrived, so when his pregnant wife came to term Amon Carter entered a frigid world. For her time and place Josephine Ream Carter was a cultivated woman. The family had a pump organ, and in later life Carter could doodle out a simple one-finger melody. But children were expected to work and work hard, and in a single day when he was seven he reportedly picked 104 pounds of cotton. He also found ways to earn odd nickels and dimes in Bowie, the nearest town. It was at age eleven that the future multi-millionaire first left home, without getting very far. Two years later, after his mother died, he gave up trying to live under the same roof with a new stepmother and departed again, permanently. Formal schooling had ended with the fifth grade.

When as a grown man, successful and rich, Carter indulged himself by sporting full Western regalia back East and shooting pistols in public places (during a Giants-Yankees World Series game, for example) he may have been making up for the early nose-to-the-grindstone days. His first jobs were menial. Typical were his labors in an 11-bed rooming house in Bowie. In return for $1.50 a week plus room and board, he did everything from waiting tables to making beds and emptying out the slops.

Hopping freight cars, Carter travelled as far as San Francisco. His first experience with an elevator took place in Fort Worth, where he made a special point of going into a building in which one of the newfangled contraptions carried him all the way to the seventh floor and down again. That may have given him a strong enough sense of Fort Worth's potential that eventually he came back to stay and become the greatest booster it—and conceivably any city anywhere—ever had.

When he was 19, Carter went on the road as a salesman for a company that capitalized on mothers' willingness to spend money for inexpensive oil paintings copied from their children's photographs. Once the paintings had been paid for, the mothers discovered they were of an unusual size that would fit only special frames, sold by the same

Navaho Women, Child and Lambs *by Laura Gilpin, platinum print, 1931.*

company and *not* inexpensive. In short order Carter was the company star and was sent all over the country, working his magic in every state of the union.

Earning a good living, he was able to marry a girl he had met in Bowie, Zetta Thomas, his first of three wives. Together they moved to San Francisco, where he had been offered a job with seeming potential in an advertising agency. This proved to be a mistake: his new income failed to keep pace with his responsibilities, which soon included a daughter. Before long they were heading again for home territory. Fort Worth was the city in which Carter set up the Texas Advertising and Manufacturing Company, a one-man operation. Luck still eluded him, and as debts accumulated, he sent Zetta and little Bertice back to Bowie to live with Zetta's parents.

Joining forces with a couple of reporters who thought Fort Worth could use another afternoon newspaper to compete with the *Telegram*, Carter next located a backer with whose help they founded the *Star*, which began publication in February 1906 with Carter as its ad salesman. This was another venture that didn't prosper. By an ironic twist the *Star* survived through Carter's persuasiveness in enlisting its original backer and others in a scheme to buy the *Telegram* and merge the two papers. The *Telegram*'s management agreed to being bought. Thus on January 1, 1909,

the *Star-Telegram* came into existence as the town's only afternoon daily. Carter had stepped again into an elevator, one destined to carry him to the posts of publisher of the *Star-Telegram*, chairman of the board of Carter Publications, Inc., and owner of the radio and television stations with the call letters WBAP.

From now on he was in a position of growing power, and, more than any other person, he is credited with broadening the industrial and business base of his community and increasing its amenities. An early flying enthusiast, he was instrumental in getting Fort Worth chosen as the site of three World War I airfields. He pulled strings to have airmail service introduced to Texas in 1925 and subsequently took all necessary steps to build his favorite city into a military, civilian, and corporate center of aviation. His philanthropies were many, sometimes anonymous. Under his direction the *Star-Telegram* enjoyed the largest circulation of any daily in Texas and wielded an influence comparable to that of any paper in the nation.

Carter was the most gregarious of men and knew and entertained the famous of the day. Noted for his hot temper, he also had a sense of humor. The rivalry between Dallas and Fort Worth, situated in adjoining counties, is a matter of record: their present airport in common had to be built exactly equidistant from both cities to be acceptable

to either, and residents of Fort Worth still react negatively when it is called—as it often is—Dallas Airport. On those occasions when Fort Worth's leading citizen had to spend the day in Dallas, he would carry his lunch with him in a brown paper bag. Some of his best friends were in Dallas, but he loved needling them. On a couple of occasions he arranged for his car to be accompanied to the county line by a police escort, sirens going full blast.

When Amon Carter died in 1955, his current wife and her two predecessors attended the funeral. He had been hard to live with, no question, but had done what he could to make up for it. After his first wife, Zetta, lost all the money he settled on her through bad investments, he saw to it that she received a regular stipend. He also helped care for his younger sister and the step-brothers and -sisters from his father's second marriage.

That his memory remains fresh today is due in considerable measure to the museum in Fort Worth bearing his name. His second and surviving daughter, Ruth Carter Stevenson, says, "If he ever set foot in a museum, I don't know about it." But in his will, providing for the creation of a building to house his collection, he refers to himself as "a part of the heritage of Texas," and says, "Its pioneer spirit that peopled the wide spaces and laid the foundations of a happy future comes down to me in the strain of the blood, and I wish to share it with others who would make Texas their home and inspiration."

Sid Richardson's career was marked by roller-coaster ups and downs, tied as it was to the wild swings of the young petroleum industry. Richardson himself was young, a 22-year-old not long out of Baylor University, when he opted for the precarious life of a wildcatter.

Richardson was born in Athens, southeast of Dallas, in 1891. Like Carter, he came into his millions only after a series of false starts and thwarted hopes. Then he lost them, made them again, lost them and, finally, ended up richer than ever.

He bought his first Russell in 1942 and continued to collect Russells and Remingtons until shortly before his death in 1959. An unreconstructed bachelor, he maintained a retreat on San Jose Island off Rockport, Texas, as well as a room in the Fort Worth Club. Carter, not the most domesticated of husbands, had a suite there, and the two men spent their free time together playing gin rummy and poker. Both of them were surrounded by their Remingtons and Russells—in Carter's case because neither his second nor third wife would allow such inelegant art at home.

Though not a public figure of high visibility, Richardson hobnobbed with state and national political leaders, particularly of the Democratic persuasion, and exerted the

Three Generations *by Charles M. Russell, oil on canvas, 17" by 24⅛", 1897.*

A Taint In The Wind *by Frederic Remington, oil on canvas, 27⅛″ by 40″, 1906.*

The Sentinel *by Frederic Remington, oil on canvas,*
34" by 49", 1889.

The Tenderfoot *by Charles M. Russell, oil on*
canvas, 14⅛" by 20⅛", 1900.

kind of influence to be expected of one in the upper eche-lons of oil and ranching. He participated in many philan-thropic undertakings, often dragooned into supporting Carter's pet causes.

Richardson had an only nephew, Perry Bass, whom he took on as a partner. Contrary to popular assumption, Bass chose not to inherit his uncle's wealth, so most of the $105-million estate went into the Sid W. Richardson Foun-dation, while trusts valued at $2.8 million each were left to Perry's four sons. Bass Brothers Enterprises today is a major financial force, and Sid, one of the brothers, and his former wife, Anne, are carrying on the Richardson tradi-tion as collectors of art—though not his kind of art. Their taste runs to modern: Morris Louis, Frank Stella, Ells-worth Kelly, Robert Irwin.

To provide a congenial permanent home for Rich-ardson's collection, the foundation trustees established a museum that occupies the ground floor of a replica of an 1895 building in downtown Fort Worth.

The 52 pictures displayed in the Richardson Collection comprise 34 Russells and 18 Remingtons. An oddity is an *Indian Head*, pencil, watercolor, and gouache on paper, executed by Russell with two friends. Indians are por-trayed more often in peaceful than warlike pursuits, though a striking canvas titled *When Blackfeet and Sioux Meet* de-picts a violent encounter between braves of these hostile tribes, two in the foreground mounted, a third unhorsed by the enemy. Russell at one point considered settling down with an Indian woman. Brian W. Dippie in his *Remington & Russell: The Sid Richardson Collection* (University of Texas Press, 1982) suggests that his *Three Generations*, which shows three generations of Indians, one of them an old crone, may express his fear of the premature aging of Indian women under their routine of ceaseless drudgery.

Russell took particular pleasure in the high jinks of cow-boys. His *The Tenderfoot* epitomizes the rough humor of the breed as a newcomer to town is forced by a hail of bullets aimed within inches of his feet to dance through an initiation ceremony.

Remington excelled in dark and shadowy effects evok-ing a sense of mystery and peril. Several of his canvases here exemplify this aspect of his art. In *A Taint in the Wind*, a stagecoach, lanterns glowing, is coming along a moonlit road. The horses and men on the coach have scented trouble and are on the alert. Something—or some-one—is about to strike. *The Sentinel*, in a lighter, bluer moonlight, with snow on the ground, captures the lone-liness of an Indian lookout, rifle athwart his horse's neck, also on the alert but facing no apparent threat.

Other Remingtons in the collection cover a wide range of subjects, from the plight of a white man taken prisoner by Indians to fast-running horses, to a bear cornered in a hunt, to a night scene of Apaches seated around a fire sing-ing a medicine song, to portraits including one of himself on a horse in a cowboy outfit. The cowboy self-image was a bit of romanticism that even the artist, increasingly disil-lusioned with the West, more and more commercialized and "civilized" during his lifetime, was unwilling to give up.

Until late 1985 the Amon Carter Museum, which opened its doors in 1961, carried a nameplate designating it the Amon Carter Museum of Western Art. With the re-moval of the plate, the last three words were dropped offi-cially from the institution's title and it became in name what it had long been in fact: a repository of American art.

Remington and Russell were the core of the original col-lection, and two of their masterpieces, the former's *A Dash for the Timber* and the latter's *Lost in a Snowstorm*, remain highlights. By board policy, two galleries always are de-voted to these artists. Works in other areas, however, change from time to time. Visitors entering the spacious main gallery today may encounter, among other things, bronze sculptures by the contemporary Elie Nadelman: a wonderful stylized horse and a man and woman doing a delicious tango. The first paintings to be seen could be by Winslow Homer, Seth Eastman, William Merritt Chase, or other eminent artists dealing with non-Western subjects.

Designed by Philip Johnson, the museum is constructed of native Texas shell stone and faces east, toward the rising sun, in the tradition of ancient Indian lodges. The five tapered arches forming its facade open onto a long porch overlooking a terraced garden and plaza. Dominating the eastern end of the plaza are abstract sculptures by Henry Moore, Upright Motives 1, 2, and 7. Displayed outside the museum, these presumably are exempted from its all-American entrance requirements.

Photographs have become an important element in the museum's holdings. In 1961, shortly after it opened, photographer Dorothea Lange wrote regarding a candid shot she had taken of Charles Russell in San Francisco in 1924 or 1926. "My question is whether you have an interest in such a documentary photograph. This is a revealing picture and should be seen and used." The museum responded by making its first purchase for a photographic collection that has since been expanded to impressive dimensions. Laura Gilpin (1891-1979), a pioneer in chronicling Southwest Indian life and gifted in other areas of photography, bequeathed her photographic estate to the museum. This consists of approximately 27,000 negatives, more than 20,000 prints, slides, and autochromes, a photographic library of some 200 volumes including rare autographed copies of books by other photographers (she herself produced four books), and extensive personal correspondence.

In addition to Gilpin, many outstanding names are represented in the photography collection. Among these are Edward Weston, Paul Strand, Imogen Cunningham, Willard Van Dyke, Charles Sheeler (who used his prints as studies for his industrial-plant paintings), Berenice Abbott, Edward Steichen, Margaret Bourke-White, and Yousuf Karsh. The oldest pieces in the collection hold enormous historical interest. An itinerant American photographer in Mexico in 1847 took daguerreotypes of the Mexican War that constitute the world's first war photographs—and very likely its first examples of photojournalism. A collotype from the mid-1840s of an Ojibway Indian called Peter Jones is the earliest known photograph of a North American Indian.

Indians were a continuing subject for photographers, some of them working for the Federal Bureau of American Ethnology. Edward S. Curtis (1907–1930) assembled a major *North American Indian Portfolio*, of which the museum has a prized copy. Civil War photographs by Alexander Gardner and George Bernard fill a significant niche, as do the pictorial records preserved by photographers accompanying government and railroad survey teams into the West in the 1860s and 1870s. Documenting conditions in

Texas for the National Child Labor Committee in 1913, Lewis Hine produced strong pictures, 64 of which are with the museum. The Depression generated an eloquent photographic testament. A complete set of prints for Dorothea Lange's Depression book *The American Country Woman* is a valued part of the collection. Under the terms of the will of Eliot Porter, renowned nature photographer and master of dye transfer color, the museum is to inherit his print, negative, and transparency files.

While many of the graphics and sculptures in the Amon Carter reflect the achievements of outstanding nineteenth-century artists, among them Saint-Gaudens, Heade, Barnett, Church, and Bierstadt, increasing attention has been paid to this century. Georgia O'Keeffe, Marsden Hartley, Arthur Dove, Grant Wood, Ben Shahn, Stuart Davis, and others are represented by some of their best canvases and works on board and paper. The energy and movement of the Remington and Russell bronzes are carried over in the more recent work of Harry Jackson, his tumultous *Stampede* conveying the danger and excitement of animals out of control.

In addition to mounting exhibitions borrowed from collections elsewhere, public and private, the museum also commissions its own, such as the controversial *In the American West* project by photographer Richard Avedon, which turned an unsparing eye on human subjects selected and posed to what some critics consider stagey effect. This show later toured the country.

A first-rate research library covering American history as well as art contains 25,000 volumes and 7,000 rolls of microfilm of nineteenth-century newspapers, U.S. and Canadian. Thanks to expansion of the building in 1977, another 60,000 books can ultimately be accommodated. This has all grown from a nucleus of some 4,000 volumes in Amon Carter's personal library.

Carter's wish "to share with others" has been fully realized, to an extent and in ways even this man of outsize ambitions could hardly have foreseen.

Storm from La Bajada Hill, New Mexico *by Laura Gilpin, gelatin silver print, 1946.*

THE MUSEUM MAKERS

Meadows:
The Second Time Around

Algur H. Meadows didn't look like an art collector, and, in fact, he made a Brobdingnagian botch of trying to be one—the first time around. Built like a football tackle and partial to loud clothes and flashy diamond cuff links, he gave the appearance of the self-made multimillionaire oil man he was. Nevertheless, he was bitten as hard by the collecting bug as any esthete, and from all the evidence he genuinely loved the kind of art he spent his money on.

In the 1950s, Meadows made frequent trips from his Dallas home base to Spain to assess that country's oil production potential. Staying at the Ritz Hotel in Madrid, he took to exploring the great museum across the plaza, the Prado. There he fell under the spell of the artists, some of them Spanish-born, others imported by royal patrons or personally drawn to the thriving, intellectually vigorous country of their day from other parts of Europe. Working with an adviser who claimed to be on the Prado's staff,

Meadows bought many examples of the kinds of paintings and drawings he had grown to admire. The adviser's connection with the Prado, as was learned later, had ended several years previously.

Eager to share his treasures, Meadows presented them to Southern Methodist University in Dallas. That institution's art department, suspecting their authenticity, advised against accepting them, but the advice went unheeded.

After his wife died, Meadows decided to honor her memory with an additional gift to SMU: a handsome structure to house the collection. The new museum, with an interior incorporating Spanish design elements of great elegance, was established on the campus in 1965. All it needed, Meadows decided, was a director. A young Ph.D. candidate in art history at New York University, William B. Jordan, was recommended. Meadows invited him and his former professor in Madrid, Don José Lopez-Rey, to come to Dallas.

The visitors went through the collection, which was supposed to contain a selection of the finest art of Spain from the sixteenth century on. Then they sat down to lunch with Meadows and told him the truth: many of the paintings earlier than the nineteenth-century were misattributed. While some were from the periods they were supposed to be, the artists were not the great names cited by Meadows' consultant.

The really great artist in this whole affair had been the con artist who, between 1951 and 1966, had palmed off probably the largest assortment of fake masterpieces ever sold to one buyer. (The same buyer also had begun collecting early twentieth-century canvases by artists such as Picasso and Modigliani, which adorned the walls of the Meadows' home. When these works were examined following the exposure of those in the museum, they too turned out to be fakes. Many were by Elmyr de Hory, the king of art forgers.)

Absorbing the bad news he had just been handed about his Spanish art, Meadows took a deep breath and asked how much it would cost to replace the imitations with the real thing. The answer: "A million dollars."

He immediately hired Jordan—a native Texan, incidentally—to run the museum and advise him on future purchases.

Jordan has since become deputy director of the Kimbell

The Meadows Museum on the campus of Southern Methodist
University houses one of the finest collections of Spanish painting
in the world. The nucleus of its holdings was assembled by Dallas
oilman Algur H. Meadows. The oil portrait of Philip IV was done
by Velazquez in 1623–24.

The Madhouse at Saragossa *by Francisco Goya, oil
on tin, 17¼" by 12¾", 1794.*

Portrait of Queen Mariana *by Diego Rodriguez de Silva Velazquez, oil on canvas, 18⅜" by 17⅛", circa 1656.*

Jacob Laying the Peeled Rods Before the Flocks of Laban, *circa 1665, by Bartolome Esteban Murillo was purchased by a farsighted curator for the museum before the artist was duly appreciated by modern-day scholars.*

Among the Meadows Museum's most important canvases is The Flaying of St. Bartholomew, *painted in 1666 by Juan Carreno de Miranda.*

Museum in Fort Worth and Meadows is dead, having lost his life in 1978 in an auto accident. But the Meadows Museum today beautifully fulfills the purpose for which it was created, both to serve an educational function and afford pleasure to students and public alike. It has pictures any museum in the world would be proud to own. That it was able to obtain certain outstanding canvases not available to the ordinary bidder was frequently due to one or more of several factors: Meadows' excellent connections with Spanish officialdom, the fact that he had in the past given pictures to the Prado, and his talent for negotiating. An important Carreño (Juan Carreño de Miranda) from 1666, *The Flaying of St. Bartholomew*, for example, was acquired through clever strategy. The Prado agreed to set a relatively modest price on the picture and arrange for an export license in return for Meadows paying a higher than usual tax on it. The tax money, being earmarked for the Prado, enabled the museum to buy a painting it particularly wanted.

Getting choice old paintings out of Spain can be a difficult business at best. Philip IV (1605–1665), generally considered an ineffectual ruler, nevertheless had a keen appreciation of art and was a passionate collector. By supporting artists of first rank, such as Velázquez, and taking possession of much of what they produced, he enriched the holdings of the crown. To this day the Spanish government retains title to a great deal of art that simply is not for sale, a situation placing obstacles in the way of collectors and encouraging the sort of sleight-of-hand practiced on Algur Meadows. What has been assembled at the Meadows Museum is thus all the more noteworthy.

During his tenure as Meadows director, William Jordan was credited with bringing in his share of bargains, thanks to an ability to see what others missed or misinterpreted. In one such instance he was permitted to take a *St. Sebastian* by Fernando Yañez de la Almedina (ca. 1506) out of Spain because everyone else thought it was by some minor Italian. Once he had got it home and had it cleaned, the painter's true identity and the worth of the painting were clearly established.

Jordan also brought Murillos when that seventeenth-century artist was held in somewhat low esteem. The very qualities that had made him popular in his lifetime—idealized beauty of countenance and gentle sentiment—led to

his being charged with sentimentality. Today he is recognized for his ability to inspire sympathy and affection for the characters portrayed and for his superior technical skill.

Spanish art may be the oldest of which we have a record, in the prehistoric cave paintings at Altamira, dating from 12,000 to 15,000 years ago. The earliest painting in the Meadows was produced during the reign of Ferdinand of Aragon and Isabella of Castile toward the end of the fifteenth century. This is a remarkable canvas in Late Gothic Style by Francisco Gallego, *Acacius and the Ten Thousand Martyrs*. Legend had it that Acacius, a Roman centurion, and his legion of 10,000 men, battling rebels in the Euphrates River area in 303 A.D., were converted to Christianity by an angelic voice, after which they swept on to victory. Subsequently, refusing to make sacrifices to idols, all were tortured, crucified, or both. Gallego's tour de force, with its forest of crucifixes to which are nailed victims clothed in elegant, predominantly red late-fifteenth-century court garb, projects an unsettling image of bright color, clashing angles, and sharply individuated bodies and faces.

That the Meadows conceives its true mission to lie in collecting what is not likely to be found in most other museums is suggested by its first major acquisition in five years, announced in 1986 and funded by a grant from the Meadows Foundation, which Algur Meadows also established before he died. This is a second canvas by Carreño, *Portrait of the Dwarf Michol*. Dwarves were popular figures in courts, and the sitter for Juan Carreño de Miranda's study, seen surrounded by lap dogs, goldfinches, and cockatoos, may have been charged with the care of such pets in the court of Charles II and Marie Louise d'Orléans. The young French queen is known to have brought cockatoos with her to Madrid, much to the chagrin of her Spanish ladies-in-waiting, who were convinced the birds were delivering themselves of indelicate remarks in French.

The Meadows Museum acknowledges gaps in its holdings, which it hopes to fill. For example, it owns little sculpture, and although it has copies and works from the school of El Greco, it owns nothing by El Greco himself. Nevertheless, by any yardstick, the museum constitutes one of the finest encyclopedic collections of Spanish painting in the world.

Miss May Sartoris *by Frederic Leighton, oil on canvas, 59⅞" by*
35½", circa 1860.

THE MUSEUM MAKERS

Dream of a Modest Man:
The Kimbell

If a novelist were to create the sort of character whose lasting legacy was one of the world's great small art museums, the portrait would probably bear slight resemblance to Kay Kimbell. Kimbell never traveled abroad ("I haven't seen all there is to see in Texas yet," he was fond of saying). He was shy and reserved in public, most at ease with his wife, business associates, and employees. He liked to spend weekends driving around the state checking up on his flour mills and comparing prices in grocery stores.

He did have an innate appreciation of art, and during the Depression, before he started accumulating his fortune, decorated his home and his office with calendar art reproductions.

Born in 1886 in Oakwood, Texas, Kimball completed the elementary grades of public school in the small North Texas town of Whitewright and at 13 went to work full time for his father. The elder Kimbell was a model of industry, active over the years as a farmer, miller, stockman, merchant, cotton dealer, and trader. To build upon the practical experience gained in his father's employ, Kimbell resumed his formal education, taking commercial courses at Grayson County Junior College in Denison.

Milling was the field to which he initially applied himself, achieving sufficient success to become head of his own operation in Sherman. In 1924 he moved his plant to Fort Worth, which served thereafter as headquarters for all his ventures which included food processing, packing, wholesaling, and, eventually, retailing, insurance, real estate, and petroleum production and processing.

With affluence came opportunity to cultivate his latent taste for art. In the 1930s, visiting a Fort Worth Art Association-sponsored show in the old downtown public library, Kimbell discovered eighteenth-century English painting. The New York dealer Bertram Newhouse, a major lender to the show, was present, and on the spot Kimbell arranged to buy one of the pictures that had particularly caught his fancy. Thereafter, Newhouse and his sons, Clyde and Ross, were to guide Mr. and Mrs. Kimbell in purchases including art of the later Renaissance, of nineteenth-century France and America, and more works of quality from England.

The role of Velma Kimbell (nee Fuller), whom he married on Christmas Eve, 1910, in Durant, Oklahoma, cannot be overlooked in an account of how Kimbell developed

The Cheat with the Ace of Clubs *by Georges de la Tour, oil on canvas, 38½" by 61½", circa 1630.*

The Raising of Lazarus *by Duccio di Buoninsegna, egg tempera and gold on wood, 17⅛″ by 18¼″, 1308–11.*

as a collector. The two never had children, and a love of art constituted one of their strongest bonds. She would often accompany him on business trips, and whenever he had two or three hours to spare they would head for the nearest museum. Later in life, they frequented galleries both in New York and California. Their home grew so rich and crowded with canvases that it became a magnet for tour groups, and special exhibitions were sent traveling to nearby colleges and universities, libraries, and churches.

It would be a mistake to portray Kay Kimbell as a man with only two main preoccupations: work and art. Throughout their life together, he and his wife were patrons of the theater. As a fan of baseball and football, especially the latter, Kimbell was to become a regular box holder at Texas Christian University football games. He also had a box at Fort Worth's annual stock show.

As he became an important man in the community, Kimbell developed friendships with those other Fort Worth art collectors, Sid Richardson and Amon Carter, though his taste differed from theirs in favoring works of more academic painters.

During the years he was acquiring art, Kimball was also making substantial contributions to charity. Neither these gifts nor the assistance he extended to individuals needing medical care or help in business were ever publicized, although some of those on the receiving end broke the silence.

To ensure that the collection he had started would be able to expand in a suitable setting, Kimbell established an art foundation. Wisely, he placed few restrictions on those who, after his death, were to oversee the construction and management of the new museum that was the foundation's raison d'être. He died in 1964, and Mrs. Kimbell did her part to further his dream by turning over her entire share of the community property to the foundation.

On the evidence of the Kimbell Art Museum both as a building and as a collection, only the finest talents were involved in its creation. The physical building, designed between 1967 and 1972, was the last completed under the personal supervision of its distinguished architect, Louis I. Kahn of Philadelphia, and may well be his masterpiece. Standing across from the Amon Carter Museum on Camp Bowie Boulevard in Fort Worth, it consists of a connected series of 16 light-filled, concrete vaults roofed with thin sheets of lead. Natural materials inside and out, such as white oak and travertine, are combined with stainless steel, aluminum, concrete, and glass. Narrow skylights with aluminum reflectors the length of the vaults diffuse natural light into the galleries. The whole effect is airy and reposeful, conducive to maximum enjoyment of the art.

Richly endowed, the Kimbell has been able to compete with larger museums as major works have come onto the market. The money on which it may draw for purchases each year is estimated at between $7 and 8 million, an amount believed second only to that available to the Getty Museum in Malibu, California. Since its opening in 1972, the museum has had only two directors: Richard F. Brown, who held the post until his death in 1979; and Edmund P. "Ted" Pillsbury, who in 1986 turned down an offer to become director of the National Gallery in London. Given the importance of the Kimbell's acquisitions, it is significant that a number of paintings bought by Kay and Velma Kimbell are good enough to hold their own among the later additions. The original Kimbell canvases include some by Frederic Leighton, Juan de Arellan, Marie Anne Elisabeth Vigée-Lebrun, Canaletto, Sir Joshua Reynolds, Thomas Gainsborough, George Romney, and Sir Thomas Lawrence.

Besides extending its representation of European art, not infrequently with the addition of an old master painting, the Kimbell has broadened its scope to take in Asia, Africa, and Central America. To avoid impinging on other Fort Worth museums, its collection does not go beyond the 1930s nor does it display American art.

Yet the Kimbell compensates for gaps elsewhere. It is the only institution in the American Southwet exhibiting Asian art in any depth, and its selections of African and Pre-Columbian pieces are choice. Outstanding among the European old master paintings for which it is especially noted are *The Cheat With the Ace of Clubs* by Georges de La Tour, Ducio's *The Raising of Lazarus*, *Portrait of Sir Thomas Le Strange* by Hans Holbein, Caravaggio's *The Card Sharp*, and other major works by Velázquez, Rembrandt, El Greco, Rubens, Fra Angelico, Bellini, Delacroix, and Goya. Among more modern paintings are those by Corot, Courbet, Manet, Monet, Picasso, Matisse, Cézanne, Mondrian, and Miró. There are also carefully chosen examples of sculpture from various periods. Besides its permanent collection, the Kimbell plays host to traveling exhibitions.

Love of art and philanthropy have rarely been combined to more felicitous effect than in this jewel of a museum. The nearest thing to it in scale, taste, and feeling may be The Menil Collection in Houston.

Portrait of an Elderly Ecclesiastic *by El Greco, oil on canvas, 42⅛" by 35½", circa 1610–14.*

The Menil: Houston's Big News

The Menil Collection, Houston, Piano & Fitzgerald, Architects East Facade.

Right: Broken Obelisk *by Barnett Newman, Cor-ten steel, 26' by 10'5" by 10'5", 1963–67.*

It is safe to assume that a visitor to Houston today going by cab to the Menil Collection will have no trouble getting delivered there. Before the new museum opened, however, anyone taking a taxi to the Rothko Chapel, another de Menil project, might well have been driven around in circles while the cabby tried to figure out where it was. The Menil Collection has established itself as big news on Houston's art scene, focusing attention on the Montrose area, an inner-city neighborhood of mostly working-class bungalows dating from the 1920s, where the collection and the chapel occupy adjacent sites.

"This museum was not built just for a group of scholars or a few collectors," Dominique de Menil, 79, told guests on opening day. "It was built for the public—for you. We hope you will come often. There will be things I am sure will enchant you, others may puzzle you, but I think with more familiarity with what looks a little bit strange you will become aware of the great qualities that are here."

Time will tell how important a role the collection will play in the lives of Houston's ordinary citizens. Many a sophisticated museum-goer from other parts has found it worth a special trip to the city, for the Menil is unusual both in the quality of its holdings and in its setting and architecture. Over a span of two decades Mrs. de Menil and, until he died in 1973, her husband John, acquired half a dozen blocks of clapboard houses in Montrose. In addition to building the Rothko Chapel here, they proceeded to convert some of the small houses to Menil Foundation offices and to renovate others and rent them out as improved residences. Retaining the basic character of the plain, timber-frame dwellings, they had them painted a uniform gray, as most had been originally. Then, when the museum came to be designed, a major requirement was that it should blend in with the surrounding buildings—an objective beautifully realized.

Dominique and John (born Jean) de Menil, both French, met at a ball in Versailles and married in 1931 when he was 27 and she 22. Of Protestant background, Dominique converted to John's Catholic faith. Her family, the Schlumbergers, had grown rich in the textile business, and her branch of it even richer when her father, a physicist, invented an electrical device for detecting oil deposits. John had been born into a military family, a titled one but poor because of his father's commitment to paying off a debt

Golconde *by Rene Magritte, oil on canvas, 31½" by 39½", 1953.*

incurred by a relative. Seven years after marrying Dominique, John joined Schlumberger Ltd., which, as a key company serving the petroleum industry, had its American headquarters in Houston. It was to this safe haven that the pair with their three children (later to become five) fled from Europe following the Nazi invasion of France. Jean Americanized himself into John, in the same spirit in which the "de" was later dropped from the names of The Menil Foundation, a funding organization for artistic, ecumenical, educational, and minority causes, and the Menil Collection.

Although Dominique has traced her collecting impulse to childhood, what she calls her "craving" for art reflects a frustrated passion of her mother's—frustrated because Schlumberger *père* disapproved of throwing money away on paintings, drawings, and the like. But it was not until the de Menils were settled in the United States and making frequent trips to New York starting in the 1940s that they began to indulge Dominique's craving. John appears to have quickly developed his own, of equal intensity. Introducing them to galleries and guiding them in their early acquisitions was a Dominican priest and painter from France, Father Marie-Alain Couturier. With his encouragement the enthusiastic novices purchased works of such modern masters as Braque, Cézanne, and Picasso. Through an influential dealer, Alexander Iolas, they became interested in surrealism, buying, among others, Klée, Brauner, de Chirico, Ernst, and Magritte. The surrealist portion of the collection is today probably unmatched anywhere in the world. Yet not everything acquired was to be of our own era or culture. As curiosity, taste, and self-confidence increased, the de Menils added sculptures, ceramics, and decorative and religious objects from over a wide historic and geographic range. The Paleolithic, Neolithic, Bronze, and Iron Ages yielded riches, as did the Cycladic period, ancient China and Egypt, and other past civilizations. Also there were paintings, tapestries, and European works of other sorts from the sixteenth to the eighteenth centuries, contemporary American art, Oceanic, American Indian, and African tribal art, and examples of the colonial arts of Latin America. While not encyclopedic, the collection as it stands is rewardingly varied.

The de Menils learned as they went along, and much of what they learned they shared with those around them. For close to 20 years, from the late 1940s on, they poured time, money, and energy into Houston's St. Thomas University with the dual purpose of furthering art education and ecumenism. The initially small institution run by the Basilian Fathers expanded in faculty, in physical size, courses, and concerns, to such an extent that the Fathers eventually questioned whether St. Thomas wasn't being changed from a Catholic to a secular school. The de Menils loosened their ties to St. Thomas, switching in 1969 to Rice University, which was secular by charter and welcomed help in the areas of liberal and fine arts. Under this new affiliation the de Menils set activities and programs in motion, with the understanding that if they proved successful, Rice would take them over. After half a dozen years a number of the seeds the benefactors had planted bore fruit, Rice was able to assume the kind of responsibility and control envisioned, and de Menil intervention was reduced. Dominique, however, continues to provide fellowships for graduate students in art history and to administer the Institute for the Arts she and her husband established.

Off campus, the de Menils promoted art and art education by becoming members of community organizations. Because of a perceived tendency on their part to try to run things their own way, they were not always welcomed by fellow members. In the 1940s, exhilarated by their discoveries under Father Couturier, they joined the Contemporary Arts Association and played an active role in mounting avant-garde exhibitions. This relationship foundered and they next turned to the Museum of Fine Arts, where John was elected a trustee. Here, conflict arose, in part because of John's determination to bring in James Johnson Sweeney, former director of the Guggenheim Museum in New York, as director. When, after a time, Sweeney was ousted, the de Menils cooled toward the museum. Probably their experiences in trying to work with others encouraged them to think of creating a facility of their own for the preservation and presentation of their collection. In any case, they were accustomed to acting independently not only in matters of art but in many other areas.

Well before Houston as a whole was ready to adopt desegregation, the de Menils were welcoming blacks to their circle—helping, in one instance, to launch the political career of Mickey Leland, a future member of Congress. During the Vietnam War they were conspicuously aligned with the peace movement. The Rothko Chapel, which preceded The Menil Collection to Montrose, and the *Broken Obelisk* standing across from its entrance bespeak the de Menils' openness to all faiths and their espousal of universal human rights. Commissioned by the couple in 1964 to create a religious environment, "a sacred place," the late Mark Rothko conceived the octagonal plan of the chapel and worked closely with the architects. In 1965 and 1966 he painted the 14 canvases for the chapel interior—richly textured but unpatterned, mostly black, with subtle shadings into burgundy and violet. Ranged around the otherwise undecorated walls of the windowless structure, illuminated

La mère et l'enfant *by Fernand Léger, oil on canvas, 36½" by 25¹¹/₁₆", 1951.*

Untitled *by Joan Miró, oil on canvas, 59⅛" by 88⅝", 1930.*

indirectly by skylights, these establish a mood of serenity, of abstraction from the world, conducive to meditation. *The Broken Obelisk* by Barnett Newman, a friend of Rothko's, was acquired in 1968, the year Martin Luther King, Jr. was assassinated, and is dedicated to his memory. Twenty-six feet high, constructed of Cor-ten steel and set in a reflecting pool, it consists of a square base plate beneath a four-sided pyramid whose tip meets and supports that of the up-ended broken obelisk. The two tips have exactly the same angle (53 degrees, borrowed from that of the Egyptian pyramids, which had long fascinated the artist), so that their juncture forms a perfect X. With its jagged, unfinished top, the vertical sculpture suggests aspiration—but aspiration deflected by the nature of human fallibility from full attainment of its goals.

One of the particularly satisfying aspects of The Menil Collection on its present site (it was temporarily housed, piecemeal, in various locations) is that the chapel and obelisk are only a block away.

To design the new building, Mrs. de Menil drew on her connection with the Pompidou Center in Paris (she heads the Georges Pompidou Art and Culture Foundation), and retained one of its architects, Renzo Piano. What she wanted for Houston, however, was something quite different from the Pompidou's brash and ebullient pseudo-industrial plant. Piano has given her a two-story 402-foot-long box of wood, glass, and steel, plain but not austere. A sense of bulkiness is avoided because the top floor is set well back from the first. An ingenious system of fixed

ferro-cement "leaves" overhead admits and filters sunlight for optimum viewing of the art. Besides covering most of the roof, the leaves extend out around the entire structure to make a covered walkway. All exhibition space is on the first floor, divided into sections, some of which contain small glassed-in gardens. Open storage of the more than 10,000 items in the collection—paintings, drawings, prints, sculpltures, photographs, books, etc.—is on the floor above, where scholars, students, and others may inspect them. Outside, a sculpture garden has taken shape since the opening.

Rotating exhibitions are drawn from the resources of the storage area. These include dramatic theme shows of a sort that Mrs. de Menil and the museum's director, Walter Hopps, were wont to produce in other settings over the years.

The building cost approximately $21 million, of which more than half was raised in contributions—$5 million each, for example, from the Brown Foundation and the Cullen Foundation. The former was established by the late George R. and Herman Brown, partners in the Brown & Root engineering-construction company; the latter by the late, oil-rich Hugh Roy Cullen. The art in the museum is estimated to be worth as much as $175 million.

With the addition of The Menil Collection to the Contemporary Arts Museum and Museum of Fine Arts, Houston can legitimately claim recognition as one of the present day's major centers of the visual arts.

Right: Capricorn *by Max Ernst, bronze, 94½" by 80⅝" by 51¼", 1948/1964.*

ACKNOWLEDGMENTS

The author is grateful to many people for their help on this book. Among them are a number who were interviewed but are not represented in the following pages. As the manuscript grew, it became evident that it would need trimming and shaping, so, metaphorically speaking, certain collections have had to end up on the cutting room floor. For this, my apologies.

It is impossible to thank by name all who have supplied information, suggested leads, opened doors, and offered hospitality, but the list must surely include Marilyn O. Allen, Mary Sue Andrews, Dr. Reuven Bar-Levav, Lois Boyd, Richard Boydstun, Michael K. Brown, Marcus B. Burke, William J. Carey, George Christian, Betty A. Coley, Catherine Craddock, Lamar Cravens, Jim DeLancey, Gene Evans, Terry Fassberg, Rose Marie Gregory, Ilse Griffith, Linda Hardberger, Clark Howard, Miriam Irwin, John J. Jasinski, Maggi Jones, E. C. Ketler, Emilie S. Kilgore, Donald E. Knaub, Ann LaPides, Owen Laster, Ginny Lewallen, Meredith Long, Wyatt McSpadden, James and Mari Michener, Ahmet Mogbel, Jane Mulkey, Marion Oettinger, Ellen G. Oppenheim, the late Dorothea Oppenheimer, James W. Phillips, Neil Printz, Hazel H. Ransom, Juliana Seeligson, Robert V. Rozelle, Elaine Steinbeck, Ruth Carter Stevenson, Alexandra Stoddard, Martha Terrill, Dale R. Terry, Decherd Turner, Ralph Webb, Vicki Vinson, and Nancy Wynne.

Special thanks to my editor, Mariana Greene, and to Dominique Gioia and others on the staff of Taylor Publishing.

INDEX

Photo Credits

p1: Hickey-Robertson
pp 14–25: Hickey-Robertson
pp 28–29: Michael Patrick
pp 30–33: Bernard Sampson
pp 34–37: David Buffington
pp 38–41: Jim Rantala
pp 42–45: David Buffington
pp 46–47: Harrah's Automobile Collection
pp 48–51: David Buffington
pp 52–55: Joe Chavanell
pp 56–59: Jim Rantala
pp 60–65: Paul G. Beswick
pp 66–67: (courtesy of Charles Tandy)
pp 68–73: Hickey-Robertson
pp 74–75: David Buffington
pp 76–77: Dwight W. Huber
pp 78–83: Joe Chavanell
p 84: Greg Hursley
pp 86–89: David Buffington
pp 90–93: Michael Patrick
pp 94–97: Jim Rantala
pp 98–101: David Buffington
pp 104–105: Michael Smith (courtesy of The Tobin Collection, McNay Art Museum, San Antonio, Texas)
p 106: McNay Art Museum, San Antonio, Texas
pp 108–111, 116: Dallas Museum of Art
p 115: Ira Montgomery
p 119: Joe Chavanell
p 121: Michael Patrick
pp 122–127: San Antonio Museum of Art
p 128: Allen Newbourn. (Courtesy of The Museum of Fine Arts, Houston)
p 129: Paul Hester. (Courtesy of The Museum of Fine Arts, Houston)
pp 130–131: Armstrong Browning Library, Waco, Texas
pp 134–137: David Buffington
pp 138–147: Hickey-Robertson
pp 148–151: T. Lindsay Baker, Editor, *Windmillers' Gazette*
pp 152–155: Paula Cooper Gallery, New York, New York
pp 156–157: Museum of Modern Art, New York, New York
pp 160–163: McSpadden Photography
pp 164–167: David Buffington
pp 168–169, 174–175: Michael Patrick
pp 170–171: Dallas Museum of Art
pp 178–181: Harry Ransom Humanities Research Center, University of Texas, Austin, Texas
pp 183–185, 191: Amon Carter Museum, Fort Worth, Texas
pp 186–189: Sid Richardson Collection, Fort Worth, Texas
pp 192–197: Algur H. Meadows Collection, Meadows Museum and Gallery, Southern Methodist University, Dallas, Texas
pp 198–203: The Kimball Museum, Fort Worth, Texas
pp 204–209: The Menil Collection, Hickey-Robertson